SILENT CRIES

Experiencing God's love after losing a baby

Jonny and Joanna Ivey

INTER-VARSITY PRESS
36 Causton Street, London SW1P 4ST, England
Email: ivp@ivpbooks.com
Website: www.ivpbooks.com

First published 2021

British Library Cataloguing-in-Publication Data
A catalogue record for this book is available from the British Library.

ISBN: 978–1–78974–142–1
eBook ISBN: 978–1–78974–143–8

1 3 5 7 9 10 8 6 4 2

Set in 11.75/15.5pt Minion Pro
Typeset in Great Britain by CRB Associates, Potterhanworth, Lincolnshire
Printed in Great Britain by Ashford Colour Press Ltd, Gosport, Hampshire

Produced on paper from sustainable forests.

*Inter-Varsity Press publishes Christian books that are true to the Bible and that
communicate the gospel, develop discipleship and strengthen the church for its mission in the
world.*

*IVP originated within the Inter-Varsity Fellowship, now the Universities and Colleges
Christian Fellowship, a student movement connecting Christian Unions in universities and
colleges throughout Great Britain, and a member movement of the International Fellowship
of Evangelical Students. Website: www.uccf.org.uk. That historic association is maintained,
and all senior IVP staff and committee members subscribe to the UCCF Basis of Faith.*

For Edith – born asleep, now awake

Contents

Acknowledgments

We would like to thank the many people who have walked the road of suffering with us since we lost our little girl, and those who were instrumental in the process of writing this book.

First of all, thank you to The Gate Church. Thank you for the way you have modelled what it means to be the body of Christ – for the cards, the nights spent weeping, the prayers, the trips to the grave, the space to grieve well together. Thank you.

Thank you to our families. To the Iveys, who have lost two of their youngest members in recent years, for all your love and support and tears. To the Ravens, where there is a heritage of tears shed for lost little ones. And to Jos, who has carried a greater burden than any child should have to. Thank you.

Thank you to our friends – you know who you are. Thank you for your constant, Christlike presence throughout our grief. Thank you for pointing us to Christ in word and deed.

Thank you to Mikaela – a fantastic midwife, whose friendship was forged in the fires of baby loss. Thank you for delivering two of our children. Thank you also to Mr Parsons – for your professional, yet personal, support throughout the anxiety and strain of subsequent pregnancies. Thank you.

Thank you to Eleanor Trotter, our editor. Thank you for backing our submission, giving us a chance to introduce others to our daughter and enabling our story to reach those who are grieving and groaning 'as in the pains of labour'.

Acknowledgments

We both want to thank Joanna's mum. Gillian to most, ShoSho to her grandchildren, we are enjoying the fruit of your faithful life now, even while you enjoy a perfected one with Jesus. Thank you, and we will see you soon.

Above all, we want to thank our faithful God, from whom we undoubtedly would have walked away, were it not for his steadfast love and faithfulness. May he use this book, however he wills, for his glory alone.

Introduction: that day

Joanna

'Your baby's big,' smiled the consultant, marking a dot towards the top of the growth chart, before rifling through a wad of maternity notes. She pulled out a sheet and scanned the numbers with her index finger. 'But it also looks like you have what we call mild polyhydramnios.' Our confused faces gave us away. 'That just means you have slightly more fluid than we'd expect. We'll need to monitor you during your final trimester, just to make sure there's nothing untoward causing it.'

While she scribbled across the notes, I noticed hanging on the wall above us a row of perspex pamphlet holders, each one embossed with a laminate label: Induction of Labour, GTT, Pre-eclampsia, DAU, C-Section Delivery. For two first-time parents, foreigners in this new world of growth charts and antenatal acronyms, it was going to require a little more than a consoling smile to keep our anxiety about the health of our baby at bay.

'What does too much fluid mean?' Jonny fumbled. 'Does it mean there could be a problem with the baby?'

The consultant smiled again: 'The majority of women with increased fluid have healthy babies . . . They have a lot of fluid, simply because they have a lot of fluid – there's no other reason for it.'

I felt a 'but' coming.

'But . . . in some cases, it's a sign that there's an abnormality in the baby's oesophagus, meaning an inability to digest the amniotic fluid properly.'

1

The word 'abnormality' was enough to distract us from the explanation of the relatively simple procedure that they'd do if this was the case.

'That's one possibility . . .' she said, reaching for a pamphlet from the GTT holder and handing it to us. 'But given the size of your baby, I'd like you to take a glucose tolerance test to find out if you're gestationally diabetic. This is relatively common in pregnancy, but because it's associated with an increased risk of stillbirth we have to manage it carefully.'

We'd wanted the bottom line, and we got it. Unsurprisingly, talk of 'malfunctions' and 'stillbirth' was enough to keep us up at night before each of those fortnightly scans. But as it turned out, Josiah was fine. Big? Yes. Protruding tummy? Well, he's his father's son. A head size that has since taken us to Birmingham Children's Hospital five times? Absolutely! But Jos turned out to be a perfectly healthy little boy, and we decided that if we never had to see another growth chart again, our world would be a happier place.

But we had no such luck . . .

When it came to our second pregnancy, we knew exactly what to expect – raised eyebrows when the sonographer measured the fluid between our little one and the wall of the uterus.

'Too much fluid?' we guessed. Correct. This pregnancy was shaping up to be exactly the same, so we weren't surprised – or anxious – to be subjected to the same process of extra scans and follow-up appointments.

There was even a nice surprise in week thirty-five when we went in for our final growth scan. We knew the routine: gel, screen, a load of weird swooshing noises. But what the midwife-sonographer said next didn't fit the routine we'd grown used to. 'Perfect! All normal.' Apparently, the fluid level had balanced out. Yes, baby – Bubs to us – was still large, but there was no diabetes, no extra fluid, no . . . nothing. Everything was normal; we could sit back and enjoy the last few weeks of the nine-month marathon!

'But remember,' the midwife continued, 'if you have any reduced movement, or any other concerns, pop back in and we'll have a look – just in case.' We nodded, excited at the thought of welcoming our little one into the world.

Later that evening, before bedtime, Bubs was wriggling around much more than usual, kicking almost constantly! At such a size, and now with only a normal amount of fluid, there wasn't a lot of space to move about in there, so each movement revealed different contours of the little body. An arm. An elbow. Toes. Such tiny toes!

Waking up next morning to our usual human alarm of Josiah announcing his hunger, we went downstairs to breakfast, a story and a prayer. For us, the day's routine had already begun. But worryingly, the littlest member of the family seemed slower than usual to start the morning.

'I don't think I've felt Bubs move this morning,' I ventured, empty teacup in hand. Jonny's brow furrowed. 'I'm sure it's fine,' I continued. 'It's just that there's usually a lot of movement at this time of day.'

During the first pregnancy with Josiah, he had twice thrown us into no small panic when he'd decided to take an in utero nap at an unusual time – so we knew the drill. I'd lie on my side, drink a glass of cold water, before playing some music to the bump. And if there was still no movement, I'd grab an ice lolly from the freezer, followed by a cup of tea. If that didn't kick-start action, it'd be a trip to the hospital, at which point Jos would decide to wake up and, to my embarrassment, kick more than usual.

'You've got a happy and healthy baby there, Mr and Mrs Ivey,' would be the default response from the midwife. But I heard it as, 'You're overreacting, Mrs Ivey.' Perhaps this was why we always feared being melodramatic.

But this time, with no movement after water, tea and an ice lolly, the midwife's words from the previous day played over in our minds: we needed to pop back into hospital, just in case.

'Are you OK?' Jonny asked from the driver's seat, a few minutes into a silent car journey. I wasn't.

'I'm OK.'

'You haven't felt anything since we left?'

I hesitated. 'Don't think so.'

Jonny knew this meant 'no'. But staring out at the morning commuters, I just didn't want to talk. I felt only numbness. *I should be on my way to work. This is all just a waste of time – it worked out fine before. Bubs is just sleeping.* But this time it felt like a particularly deep sleep.

When we arrived and went into emergency triage, we sat down next to women who looked equally nervous. A little boy played with an abacus in the corner of the waiting room, while *Good Morning Britain* provided an ironic distraction for all of us in that waiting room – frankly, our mornings had been anything but good. I chose to distract myself by thinking about the amount of work and the meetings I was missing that morning. Piers Morgan's quizzing of some politician felt like the last thing I needed.

'Joanna Ivey,' called a voice from around the corner. A small, middle-aged midwife stood waiting.

'Don't worry, love,' she said, as we went through a set of double doors and into Triage Room 3. Our anxious faces spoke volumes. As I got up on to the bed, she reached over for a grey Doppler stick attached to a heart-rate monitor. 'Let's see what this little one's up to, shall we?'

She pushed her glasses up her nose and wheeled herself towards me. I wanted to say, 'No, don't do it. Let me go home, this isn't happening.' But the Doppler made contact with my tummy and I looked ahead at the wall.

After what felt like an eternity, we heard . . .

Nothing. No heartbeat. No swooshing. Silence.

The pressure from the morning rolled quietly down my cheeks in wet tears and adrenaline invaded my face.

'No . . .' whispered Jonny, clearly assuming the worst, trying to find some air.

'Don't worry, dear, sometimes the heartbeat can take a while to find,' our midwife reassured, moving the Doppler to the other side of my bump. 'OK, we're going to need to do a scan,' she said, removing her glasses, now herself visibly flustered.

She took us immediately to a scan room opposite, where a midwife-sonographer was already waiting. Hauling your thirty-five-week pregnant body on to the bed is far harder when you're shaking with fear. But within seconds the image emerged on the screen – that grainy outline of our little one, the same image we'd seen less than twenty-four hours before. Hours and days had lost all meaning; we were somehow outside of time, like soldiers on high alert in the trenches, watching horrified as a pinless grenade landed unannounced in our bunker. Those seconds were enough to see what was coming, and to embrace – even enjoy – a fleeting moment of peace before the inevitable. I could have stayed there for ever.

'I'm so sorry,' said the midwife-sonographer. 'I can't find a heartbeat.'

The grenade had exploded.

Looking at our lifeless child, floating upside down in my womb, our own hearts also seemed to have stopped beating. Falling on each other, we wept until we wailed loudly. And when words finally did come, all we could manage was a feeble: 'What on earth do we do now?' and 'Why is nobody talking about this?'

PART 1: WEEPING

PART 2: WALKING

PART 3: WAITING

'Sun and moon'

by Ben Moore

Received on That Day, 18 September 2018

Oh friends,
Oh brother and sister,
Sometimes I'd like to tell the sun
It's not supposed to shine
On days like this.

Mourning feels like the moon's domain,
And yet, the sun insists
On coming up again each morning
To warm and light,
And banish night,
Whether we notice or not,
It gives us life.

You are walking the darkest of roads,
The pain of which I cannot know,
But I know you're not alone.

Oh friends, be weak,
Be weak and broken,
And remember, when the grief
Is too deep to be spoken,
Our God knows it,
And our Lord felt it.

Oh friends,
Oh brother and sister,
Be weak.
You don't need to be strong,
You don't even need to speak.
Death is not an enemy you are called to defeat,
And for your little one,
The sun has risen.
Just a little sooner than we'd choose.[1]

1

The happy-ever-before

Joanna

Before tying the knot, I wasn't exactly known for my organizational skills. But since marrying Jonny – someone who could make a Filofax feel disorganized – I've grown to love a good plan.

Together we thought we had it all mapped out: Josiah, our first, had just turned one, and we wanted a two-year gap between him and our number two. First time round it took us five months to conceive, so January sounded like a good time to begin trying . . . or so we thought.

'Which one shall I get, then?' asked Jonny, before clearly dropping his phone on the supermarket floor. Waiting for the rustles on the other end of the line to finish, I opened our curtains to a layer of February frost and an icy-blue sky. 'There's the expensive one, which gives you a "Pregnant" or "Not Pregnant", or there's the cheap one, which gives you one or two lines.'

'I think we'll manage with the lines. Come home soon, won't you?'

'I'll be home in five.'

After taking the test, I had to check six times that two lines really meant 'pregnant', immediately regretting my decision not to get the more expensive version. We both fell back on the bed, not knowing what to say. After struggling with those months of disappointment when trying for Jos, we couldn't believe it had all happened so quickly. Two kids under two? God must have a sense of humour! But we were over the moon, and Jonny knew exactly how to treat me – with a trip to our local McDonald's for some nuggets and fries. We Iveys really know how to celebrate!

This good news about our second child came at an otherwise difficult time. My mum had had terminal cancer for three years, and her health had recently deteriorated. The first trimester of my pregnancy was spent carting a one-and-a-half-year-old from Birmingham to Sheffield and back, in order to spend precious limited time with her. In all the busyness, I hardly had space to think about that little life tucked away inside me. At least, not until I was ten weeks pregnant.

'Jonny, come here!' I shouted from the bathroom, minutes before our church members would descend on our house for a prayer meeting. He caught the tone of my voice and ran upstairs. 'I've had some blood,' I said, tears welling up. Jonny hugged me, silent. We both knew what this meant because it hadn't been long since Jonny's sister had also had some blood. It meant miscarriage – a word so brutally cold and indiscriminately clinical. The exciting news of our second child, shining some welcome light into cancer's darkness, now looked to be extinguished. We sat on the carpet in silence . . . until the doorbell sounded.

'We can't have prayer here tonight,' said Jonny, glancing disbelievingly at his watch. 'But what do I say? Shall I just tell them what's happened or should we keep it to ourselves until we know for sure?'

My head was too full of questions to think straight. But Jonny was already downstairs, the door open.

'Hello!' came a male voice, almost certainly our friend David. And in the silence that followed, I could hear Jonny's words failing him, the rustle of a coat extending its comforting arms and, finally, the sobering sound of my husband sobbing.

'We think we've lost the baby . . .' – just hearing those words from upstairs made me feel sick in the pit of my stomach – 'It looks like Joanna's miscarrying.'

That evening, the relocated prayer evening became a time of pleading with God for our ten-week-old baby. While the church prayed, we managed to get a late-night appointment with a GP, but she gave no reassurance.

'Yes, it sounds like miscarriage. But don't worry; it's really common in the first trimester – one in four, they reckon,' she said, writing up notes on the computer. 'I'll book you in for a scan at the hospital to confirm it, but I suspect this won't be for a couple of days.'

I was dumbstruck. Since when was something so awful made 'OK' because of how common it was? This *wasn't* OK. Common or not, this wasn't natural or normal. This was unimaginable. This couldn't be happening – but the continuing loss of blood stated otherwise.

On the way home, I'd run out of tears. 'I feel so guilty,' I whispered through silent cries. 'I haven't had the time to think about the baby at all with everything that's going on with Mum. And now our baby's gone.'

'We don't know that yet, sweetheart,' Jonny replied, though I could tell by his voice that he didn't have much hope either.

As we pulled up to a red traffic light, he put his hand on my knee and turned to me.

'It just feels like . . . like there's so much death . . .' I said, closing tired eyes. 'Why is our baby dying too?'

Jonny

The day before the scan, we lay on our bed, unable to work or even eat. A slice of sunlight escaped through a gap in the curtains and the alarm clock ticked in my left ear. Empty teacups and chocolate wrappers flanked the bed where Joanna sat propped up by a mountain of cushions. I lay flat, staring at the white ceiling. Like watching a car crash in slow motion, our powerlessness to stop what was happening seemed to taunt us.

As a result of my sister's miscarriage we already knew the shocking statistics about how many children are lost to powerless parents, but it didn't soften the blow at all. Turning towards Joanna, I looked at her raised womb – that mysterious incubator of life – and longed to know what was happening inside. Any optimism from the previous day had begun to feel like naivety, and the more we held on to hope, the more we were putting our hearts on the line to be crushed.

However, despite all our ignorance and confusion, one thing was crystal clear: whether alive or not, it wasn't a foetus we were losing, but our precious baby. This wasn't an embryo, but a person. I thought back to all the evenings spent with Joanna poring over our pregnancy app, reading about the beating heart at only five weeks, the vital organs functioning by week nine, and the eyes moving from side to side at just a few days. These milestones, which had previously brought so much excitement, served only as a reminder of what we were losing. The healthcare professionals might call it 'pregnancy loss'. But we weren't grieving the possible loss of pregnancy; we were grieving the possible loss of our son or daughter.

That night, Joanna fell asleep early but my eyes remained firmly fixed on the ceiling. I thought about what our child might be like. *Boy or girl? Would he look like Jos? What would she make of her older brother? What would it be like having two under two?* As I lay awake, the thought that we might never know the answers made the possibility of miscarriage feel like a pressing weight, pinning me to the mattress. With no hope of falling asleep, I had to get up and move around.

Walking across the landing, I saw Josiah's bedroom door was ajar. I could hear his deep-sleep breathing and felt the urge to go in, simply to look at him. Under the glow of his nursery thermometer, he lay peacefully on his back surrounded by a sea of cuddly toys. He was clutching at the Gruffalo, his chest moving slowly up and down under his sleeping bag, the stream of life flowing rhythmically through his little body. Perhaps for the first time, I noticed the detail of his hands and of his nose, the slight glisten of his brow. This beautiful, blond boy was what ten-week-old babies become.

Creeping out of his room and into the study next door, I flicked the desk light on and pulled my leather-bound Bible from the shelf. I knew some passages about babies in the womb, but never before had I been so hungry for them. I flicked to King David's famous psalm and whispered the words out loud:

For you created my inmost being;
  you knit me together in my mother's womb.
I praise you because I am fearfully and wonderfully
    made;
  your works are wonderful,
  I know that full well.
My frame was not hidden from you
  when I was made in the secret place,
  when I was woven together in the depths of the
    earth.
Your eyes saw my unformed body;
  all the days ordained for me were written in your
    book,
  before one of them came to be.
How precious to me are your thoughts, God!

Such knowledge is too wonderful for me,
  too lofty for me to attain.
(Psalm 139:13–17, 6)

This child had been intricately formed. God had spent time thinking about the uniqueness of our baby, weaving our new child together with great care to ensure this individual resembled his own reflection in a way that only she or he could. Whatever our baby's fate, this child was not biological tissue, but was unthinkably valuable to God – as valuable as every other person in his world. Why else would he fearfully and painstakingly weave together every detail? Thinking about how much God cared for this little life, about how fully he *knew* our baby, provided spiritual balm, as I longed to know every one of those details myself. But even if we never met our son or daughter in this life, this child was no less known than the rest of us. The all-knowing God knew and loved him or her deeply.

Under the warm light of my desk lamp, the words on the page came alive. Not only had God formed our baby's physical frame but he'd also formed a plan for his or her life. All of this child's days were written in God's book before day one had even begun. I wasn't responsible for this life, because it was God's work. Yesterday and today were in the script, and so was tomorrow, whatever it would bring.

It seemed cruel that God would give so few days to our precious baby. But, confronted with a God who knew and loved this child more than I did, the angry objections of my heart were rightly stilled. Could I possibly grasp why he, so full of love, might plan it this way? King David was right: 'Such knowledge is too lofty for me to attain.' I couldn't know all the answers but, through David's psalm, God had validated my pain. The pre-emptive grief that I was experiencing for my child found its source in God's eternal love for this little life. So I wasn't being melodramatic about losing an embryo, and this really wasn't 'OK'. The life of our baby was supremely valuable, so much so that God held him or her in his hands. He'd planned the number and detail of his or her every day, and tomorrow we'd find out whether his plan gave us any more time with our younger child, so dearly and eternally loved.

Joanna

When we arrived at the Early Pregnancy Unit, I swallowed a lump in my throat as we passed the Quiet Room, with paintings of coastal scenes and boxes of tissues. The walls of the waiting room were plastered with posters from the baby-loss charity Tommy's, and a tatty water dispenser stood forlornly in the corner.

As we sat down next to piles of *Woman's Weekly*, a cloud of fear hung over the day's cohort of women and their partners who switched between Facebook on their phones and *This Morning* on TV. Women were called one by one, followed by a ten-minute gap after which they would reappear, either with a beaming smile or with sobs of disbelief.

'It feels like a lottery,' I whispered, staring blankly at the TV screen above us. Jonny didn't respond, as if he hadn't heard.

'They're an hour late,' he said eventually. 'That couple's been in there for ages now – it must be bad news.'

I sighed, breathing out the tension that my heart rate was struggling to control. The longer we waited, the more I wanted to run away from the burden of increasing guilt. *What did I do to cause this? What if I'd spent more time thinking about the baby? What if I hadn't gone to Sheffield so much, stretching myself to the limit?*

'Joanna Ivey.'

A small, dark-haired midwife was smiling – 'Claire', her name badge read.

'Would you like to come through, dear?' Claire's warmth made the floodwaters of emotion lean heavily against the dam of what's seen as socially acceptable. I climbed on to the bed, knowing as I did so that I didn't have to keep up this front for much longer.

'Sweetheart,' Claire said, picking up the bottle of gel, 'I'm going to begin with the screen turned away from you – I hope you understand.'

We understood.

She took hold of the ultrasound equipment and pulled the display monitor towards her. Jonny sat, head in hands, looking at the floor, waiting. As she pressed against my tummy, the seconds ticked. And ticked. And ticked . . .

'There we are!' Claire smiled, turning the screen towards us. Jonny looked at the ceiling and breathed out deeply. I laughed through tears, the pent-up pressure finally finding release.

'Can you see that flurry of movement?' Claire asked, pointing to a flickering seed on the screen. 'That's a little heart beating away. Here are the arms and legs. Everything looks absolutely fine.'

The life that had consumed our thoughts and fears for two days was now right there in front of our eyes. That *beat, beat, beat* of the heart – here was the sign that God had heard our silent cries and had done what we were powerless to do. He had sustained the life of our baby. Our little one was alive.

There's a photo in our living room taken in Spain, a few months after that miscarriage scare. I'm standing in a kids' pool, holding Josiah's hand, with my other hand on my second-trimester bump. I remember the gratitude we felt on that holiday, knowing that so many women don't receive the good news we heard that day – or at their twelve- or twenty-week scan. On track towards welcoming our miracle child into the world, our oblivious smiles beamed as brightly as the Spanish sun – smiles that, looking back, now haunt us.

This was the last family photo where our happy-ever-after still felt within reach. A few days after returning home, I got the call from Dad that I knew would come one day.

'Love, your mum and I have been up all night. Mum's been in so much pain that we had to call an ambulance and she's now in hospital.' Jonny flashed me a knowing look. 'The doctors aren't sure, but she might have as little as four weeks left.'

However prepared I was to hear the news, it pulled the rug from beneath my feet. 'OK . . . OK . . . OK,' was all I could manage, to reassure Dad that I was still on the line. 'We'll be there tomorrow.'

What I'd always feared was happening: Mum was going to die before meeting our baby.

Sitting next to the woman who once carried me, her second child, I held her hand, thinking about my second child. Perhaps this baby too would one day sit next to me on my deathbed and hold my hand. The starkness of life and death came into focus. It felt precious somehow . . . profound. How could I look into the eyes of the woman who'd brought me up, who'd taught me what I know about the world, who'd shown me Jesus and lived for him, who'd prayed with me, who'd argued and cried with me, who'd *loved* me – how could I look into the eyes of my dying mother and not feel the burden of responsibility for the life that I was now carrying?

'Mum – we weren't going to tell anybody the names we've chosen for the baby but, just in case . . .' I stopped, not knowing how to finish. 'Well, we just wanted you to know.'

'Oh yes, I'd love to know, darling. I won't tell Dad,' she promised. I stroked her hand, swallowing hard. Mum sat up slightly, refastening the drainage tube in her nose.

'If it's a boy, he'll be called Asher Bear Ivey.' Saying it out loud felt good.

'Oh, OK. Asher's nice,' she replied. Mum was never able to pretend she liked something if she didn't. 'And if it's a girl?'

'Edith Joy.'

'That's pretty, my love,' she whispered. 'Edith Joy.' It sounded even prettier hearing someone else say it out loud, but the thought of never hearing Mum say it as she held our daughter in her arms felt too much. I so desperately wanted her to meet our baby. What we never expected was that, of us all, Mum was going to be the first to do so.

'Winter'

by Sally Lloyd-Jones

In the winter it looks like the trees have all died. Their leaves wither and drop off. They stand like skeletons against the cold, desolate sky.

But did you know before even a single leaf falls to the ground, next spring's bud is ready? Next summer's leaf is furled inside that tiny bud, waiting.[2]

2

Groaning as in the pains of childbirth

Jonny

They say that life can be turned upside down in a heartbeat, and they're right. Not even twenty-four hours after a 'perfect' scan showing our little one kicking away, our baby's heart had beaten its last and our lives would never be the same again. Yet this baby would always be our miracle child.

When we managed to tear our disbelieving eyes away from the ultrasound image, a midwife led us out of the room, down a familiar-looking corridor and past delivery rooms where women screamed in pain.

'That's the room where Jos was born,' I said to Joanna, motioning towards a door on our left, ajar. She peered inside, but didn't say anything. It felt impossible that this was the same place where we had enjoyed one of our very best memories; now it was the stage for what was set to be our very worst.

Turning the corner at the end of the corridor, we entered the Abby Suite – a designated space for bereaved parents. Checking it was free, the midwife welcomed us into Abby Suite 2 and gave us some space to cry together. With its cream walls, soft purple furnishings and a bed, this room felt like a parallel universe. We looked out on a brick wall two yards from the window, and with craned necks, could only just make out the grey sky.

Was this the same sky that had always hung above us? Was this the same world as the one we had woken up to this morning? It felt darker. *Heavier.* Changed for good. I wanted to go back to the safe world of smiling midwives and expectant friends asking Joanna how long she had left over a post-church coffee. Now it was just Joanna, me and our baby, who'd grown so painfully still.

'Lord, we know you're able to do a miracle,' I prayed. 'Please, if you're willing, raise this child from the dead. *Please.*' I couldn't take my eyes off Joanna's bump – that rounded metaphor of new life that now housed not life but death. In some strange way, it felt confusing that the baby was still in there, as if death should have caused a sudden disappearance.

'*Not* in there,' Joanna said. 'The body's still there, but *our baby* isn't.'

She was right, of course, but somehow, we'd have to get our baby's body out – a thought that I couldn't yet get my head around. Presumably they'd just do a C-section? Surely that was best for everyone?

The door handle clicked and the midwife came and sat on the bed opposite us, followed by a doctor, who remained standing. He nodded supportively while the midwife explained the unimaginable: we'd have to come back to the Abby Suite in a couple of days for Joanna to be induced into normal labour. Just the word 'labour' conjured up images of pain, giving birth to joy and new life. In this case, Joanna's pain would give birth to more pain, then to death.

Joanna

Two days later, we arrived back at the hospital. I was surprised that, alongside the grief, I also felt some excitement. This was supposed to be the worst day of our lives, but we'd come to know and love our little one over eight months and today we'd finally meet that special person. I was resolved, but nervous, remembering the pain and problems of labour from last time. Packed in our overnight bag were two sleep suits – green trains if it was Asher, and coral foxes if it was Edith.

Walking past other pregnant women, and even some who'd just given birth, scenes of family life reeled through my mind. Weekend breakfasts and trips to the park, school runs and country walks, holidays and bonfire nights. The future we'd lost couldn't be packed into that overnight bag or into the twenty-four hours ahead of us. But we were here, not only to do a job but also to make the most of the precious little time we had to spend with our baby.

We walked up to the front desk, to two smiling receptionists.

'How can I help?' asked the one, while the other continued to file away pregnancy notes. Her mundane question caught me completely off guard.

'We're here . . . well, I've come to give birth – my baby died on Tuesday,' I stuttered. The receptionist squeezed her lips and brow together sympathetically and let us through the double doors. We clutched each other's hands tightly as we walked down the long corridor and into the Abby Suite, where one of the midwives greeted us – 'Mikaela', her name badge read.

Leading us into Delivery Room 11, Mikaela explained frankly what was about to happen; she had a thick West-country accent. However, because she said nothing about the baby, I wondered if she knew that this was a stillbirth situation. There was something about her straight-up tone, though, that endeared her to me – as though I was chatting with a friend over coffee, while doing the hardest thing I'd ever have to do.

As Mikaela left us to unpack and gather our thoughts, the room's hot air sat heavily on our shoulders. Intended to provide a warm welcome into the world, this felt pointless, given that our little one would be born cold. Apart from the heat, the room was actually very welcoming. Mikaela had brought through the aromatherapy diffuser with some lavender oil, and dim-coloured lights alternated between soft purples and crisp greens. I could hear the distant sound of water quietly filling the birthing pool.

I took a seat on a small sofa next to the bed, while Jonny began to unpack my labour bag.

'People are praying,' he said, finding space on the side for various glucose products that might be called on. 'This feels doable in a way that it didn't yesterday. God's holding us, my love.'

'I'm really grateful they've let me have a water birth,' I agreed, not knowing that this would be the hospital's first-ever stillbirth in a pool. 'Do you think our midwife knows that it's a stillbirth?'

Before Jonny had time to respond, the door opened and Mikaela slid in, unwrapping a foiled pessary.

'You might be interested to know that I've just seen a woman on the induction suite whose stillborn baby I delivered last year. I thought that might be encouraging for you.'

It really was. For some strange reason, the screams of labour coming from all around us didn't fill us with despair; they filled us with the encouragement that babies *are* born healthy and we too could be back in a year to have a living baby delivered. But despite that encouragement, we were here for *this* baby – *our* baby, no less precious than any future child. This was the place where our little one would be born and so it wasn't the scene of a horror show, it was precious. Perhaps God would even do a miracle. But this wasn't the situation in front of me, so I began preparing myself to do what no mother should ever have to do.

Mikaela gave me the induction pessary. She said that contractions could start within the next twelve hours, so when the lunch menu came round, immediately afterwards, I didn't expect that small surges would already be making it difficult to get even the smallest slice of quiche down.

Within an hour, I was breathing heavily through searing pangs. The emotional pain added a layer to the agony, which felt like it could crush me at any time. I reached for the birthing ball, got on my knees and lay with my upper body over the ball, waiting for another contraction to loosen. I couldn't let this crushing weight defeat my resolve; this was the only thing I could do for my baby. I wasn't going to be able to do what every mum should do for her child. I'd never look after this child, put dinner on the table, read bedtime stories, bath her, take him to school, just be Mum. The only thing I had to offer, and the only way I could sacrificially serve my baby, was *this* – the pain of labour, bringing this child into the world safely and with dignity. But the physical agony was becoming indistinguishable from the emotional torment; I felt I was letting my little one down in the one thing I could do for him or her. And after an hour of trying to patch up cracks in my resolve, my hope of getting through this began to collapse.

'I can't do it,' I whispered. 'I can't do it for the baby, Jonny.'

'You *can* do it, my love. God's with you; he'll get you through this. You *can* do it,' Jonny replied, rubbing my back. I thought of all the ways I'd normally need to rely on God for strength over the course of this baby's life – every health scare, every argument, every ounce of patience and prayer that would go into raising this child. And I asked God to help me channel it into that one moment of need. From our labour playlist, the minor chords and searching violins of Arvo Pärt's *Spiegel im Spiegel* played in the background between gasps and groans. I had memorized a Bible verse, which God brought to mind as I searched for any remaining shred of energy:

We know that the whole creation has been groaning as in the pains of childbirth right up to the present time. Not only so, but we ourselves, who have the firstfruits of the Spirit, groan inwardly as we wait eagerly for our adoption to sonship, the redemption of our bodies. (Romans 8:22–23)

The metaphor wasn't lost on me. As I moaned and gasped and endured, here was God's picture of how painful it is to live in a world of sin and death. My suffering was the clearest picture of any of this cursed world, where babies die and where mums have to take into their arms the silent bodies of their own children. My groans were not only physical and emotional; I was *spiritually* groaning while waiting eagerly for the redemption of my body, when I would inherit the new creation that God has promised me. And not only me, but everyone else who has fled the suffering and sin of this present age by taking refuge in Jesus. But in the meantime, we have to wait patiently, pushing through the pain.

This baby was coming soon, so I could just about push through the pain for a little longer. Mikaela said it was time to get in the birthing pool, and Jonny held my hand as I heaved and cried and panted my way over. The soft purple lights flickered to royal blues and burnt oranges, and the pool's tap kept running as I got in. Starting to feel the baby coming, I was hit by an onslaught of questions: *What does a stillborn baby look like? Would I be able to look at the baby? Would I be able to hold my child?* But before seeing what this little one looked like, I knew one thing for certain: that I loved him or her. Beyond anything else, I knew this was someone I loved dearly and longed to meet. And I wasn't far from doing so now.

After what felt like hours of pushing in the pool, the tone of Mikaela's voice and the look on Jonny's face intensified. 'You can do this – just a couple more pushes!' Mikaela encouraged. 'The head's coming; it's coming now!'

I winced and screamed and pushed this precious person out of the home I had provided for so long, and into Mikaela's arms. Jonny's face fell into his chest before looking up again and into my eyes.

'Joanna, it's Edith,' he wept. 'We have a little girl. She's such a beautiful little girl . . .'

Mikaela put Edith Joy into my arms, a moment so grave and complex that no tears welled up, as though unfit for purpose. The weight of Edith's body pressed against mine and her left cheek bunched against my shoulder. She was so . . . real. She looked like any other baby. Edith wasn't a corpse or a foetus – she was a person. An amazing creation, fearfully

31

and wonderfully made. She had chunky cheeks and a sturdy build, just like her brother. Her eyelids were soft, her veins visible. I took her by the hand and looked at the fingerprint that, one day, the library would use so she could take out books. She had big feet, which would cause her embarrassment as a teenager. Edith had my auburn hair that, maybe like me, she'd one day dye. Her eyes were blue; her brow, furrowed and blonde. She had sassy little lips which spoke loud and clear, 'Mum, Dad – I'm the naughty one.' But she kept her words to herself.

Apart from the plan and purpose of God, Edith Joy would one day giggle when we played peek-a-boo. Her name would be called out on a register on her first day at school. She would feel nervous when she didn't know an answer in her SATs exam. Edith would tell you what job she hoped to do, and what home she one day wanted to live in. Would she get married? Have children? I wonder if her children would have those same sassy lips. I liked to think so.

As cries of new life came from next door, the minor piano chords and violins continued to soothe our room's silence. I tried to imagine what Edith's cries would have sounded like, but for us they were silent. We held her so tightly, just as God holds his children, both in life and in death. I didn't feel I could put her down – ever.

Before putting on her fox sleep suit, we put a vest on her that a group of friends and I had previously made for Jos. It had the words of Jeremiah 1:5 written on it: 'Before I formed you in the womb I knew you; before you were born I set you apart.' These words were true for Jos, but they came alive as we saw Edith wearing them across her tiny chest. The Lord had planned each day for our little girl before taking her to be with him. We knew where she was. For us, her silence was the groaning of this fallen world. But to the company of heaven, it was shouts of joy from another little one who was born more alive than the rest of us. I held her cold body, praying the Lord would revive her, but I knew she was in the warmth of his arms.

Please, Lord. Though not my will, but yours, be done.

Jonny

We were transferred to Abby Suite 2, a room that felt so obviously familiar, but at the same time a world apart from when we had last sat within its cream walls. Now our baby wasn't an unknown body to get out of Joanna's womb: her name was Edith, and over the next twenty-four hours we would be privileged to look after her. To parent her, even.

We filled a baby bath with warm water and I gently washed Edith's skin while Joanna held beneath her underarms. After wrapping her in a towel, we dressed her, being careful with her delicate arms as we fed them through fresh sleeves. As Joanna supported her head and lifeless body on her lap, we opened one of her brother's favourite books, and we read to her a small passage called 'Winter', by Sally Lloyd-Jones.

In the winter it looks like the trees have all died. Their leaves wither and drop off. They stand like skeletons against the cold, desolate sky.

But did you know before even a single leaf falls to the ground, next spring's bud is ready? Next summer's leaf is furled inside that tiny bud, waiting.

And Jesus says there is nothing broken that won't be mended, nothing sick that won't be healed, nothing dead that won't live again. Because God is making everything sad come untrue!

We can't see it now – but remember the fruit tree in winter? It looks dead. But the buds are ready to go. And come spring – blossom fruit![3]

While it was a privilege to care for Edith, we weren't playing a game of make-believe, pretending she was still with us. Like a fallen leaf in winter, Edith lay dead in her wintry, refrigerated cot. She wasn't there and yet, in the same way as next summer's leaf is furled inside a tiny bud, so too was an eternal summer furled inside her tiny body. Jesus says there's nothing dead that won't live again, and that death is necessary to give birth to new life. We weren't bathing her and singing to her and reading to her because we wanted to deceive ourselves into thinking she was somehow there with us. We did these things as an earthly reminder that, beyond the walls of Abby Suite 2, there was more going on than met the eye. While Edith really had died, in the courts of heaven she was very much alive.

As I sat on the bed with Edith resting silently on top of my legs, head tilted to one side, I wasn't able to articulate the strange mix of emotions. The sadness was overwhelming, looking into her eyes, knowing that in this world they'd never fix on to mine. I despised this cursed world of death and decay, so much so that I found in myself a longing for Jesus to come and make all things new – for him to bring me into his kingdom. But the thought that Edith was already with him, that she had by-passed this world of trips to the Early Pregnancy Unit and miscarriage and stillbirth – the world of bullying and sickness and spiritual warfare and fear and depression and cancer – to think that she had gone straight to be where I longed to go, meant that I felt a surprising joy, mixed in with all the sadness.

In that confusing moment, I again turned to King David. When Bathsheba conceived his son, the truths he'd penned years earlier must have flooded back. God had intricately woven his little boy together and knew him completely. But days after he was born, he became critically ill.

> David pleaded with God for the child. He fasted and spent the nights lying in sackcloth on the ground. The elders of his household stood beside him to get him up from the ground, but he refused, and he would not eat any food with them.
> (2 Samuel 12:16–17)

Next door was the High Dependency Unit, where very sick babies were being born as we held our Edith. Christian or not, I could imagine parents praying like David for God to protect their little ones and keep death at bay. For King David, though, the sickness was too much for his son, and God took his little one. While I'm sure his grief continued for the rest of his life, his reaction to his son's death was curious, as he got up off the ground and washed. He broke his fast. And perhaps most confusingly, he went to the house of the Lord to worship the God who didn't seem to have answered his prayers. David explains:

While the child was still alive, I fasted and wept. I thought, 'Who knows? The LORD may be gracious to me and let the child live.' But now that he is dead, why should I go on fasting? Can I bring him back again? (2 Samuel 12:22–23)

On the face of it, this wasn't someone I could relate to in my own grief. But it was clear that he'd been comforted by the same timeless truth that explained the surprising sense of joy I felt in the pain. 'I will go to him, but he will not return to me' (2 Samuel 12:23b).

Despite centuries separating us, I shared with David that one glimmer of hope breaking through my despair. Edith wouldn't come back to me, but I would go to be with her in God's kingdom. David, God's own king, knew what I and millions of grieving parents around the world instinctively know to be true: that our babies have died and immediately entered the everlasting glory of heaven. And while the grief must have continued for David, as it would do for me, this was enough for him to lift his weary hands, not only to eat bread but also to worship the God who, as his forefather Abraham put it, will only do what is right (Genesis 18:25).

I walked Edith back to her cold-cot, supporting her neck as I put her down. That surprising joy amid the sadness grew as I thought of King David's unmoving faith in the character of God. His was a God who punishes wilful rejection and conscious sin against him (2 Corinthians 5:10), but who doesn't eternally condemn children on no other basis than an inherited sinful nature. Before entering the Promised Land, this God judged his people's blatant mistrust of his goodness, but spared the children because they were not yet morally culpable: 'Your children who do not yet know good from bad – they will enter the land. I will give it to them and they will take possession of it' (Deuteronomy 1:39). And if moral ignorance spares older children from God's judgment, how much more our miscarried or stillborn children?

Bent over Edith's cot, still longing for her eyes to meet mine, a tear rolled down my cheek on to hers. Nothing could take away the pain, but David's God was, and is, my God – the true and living God of heaven and earth. And so, as much as I wanted to hear Edith's giggle and see her smile, I was learning David's confidence in the God who'd taken her away to enjoy more laughter and smiles than she'd ever experience here with us.

That is what God had done for every child who'd died in the womb or in infancy. Right now, David's son, my daughter and millions, maybe billions, of children are enjoying the glorious presence of God, along with every other person who has ever been saved by the precious blood of Jesus, God's Son. I stroked her hair and smiled, wondering what she was doing up there.

One day, just as we'll see God face to face, we'll see Edith, with her beautifully resurrected body (1 Corinthians 15:42). Her eyes won't be closed any more, her limbs lifeless or her tongue quiet. And beyond what our eyes could see, all of this was true in Abby Suite 2. God had ordained 247 days, and no more, for us to enjoy that beautiful little girl. Then he whisked her into eternal joy.

People speak of our loss, and they're right to do so. But we like to speak of our gain. God gave us the gift of a daughter, so we added Adeah as a third name, which is Swahili for 'gift of God'. It is our privilege to suffer in this fallen world, in order that she would enjoy the world that we're groaning for, as in the pains of childbirth.

We'd so longed for her soul to enrich our lives, but that soul now fills the courts of heaven, which makes our grief bearable. Like David, we can eat, knowing that one day Jesus himself will serve us at God's Great Banquet (Luke 12:37). Like David, despite our grief and confusion, we can even praise this great God, who we'll spend eternity worshipping alongside our precious daughter, Edith Joy Adeah – God's gift to us.

3

Goodbye, little one

Jonny

Waking up the next morning, I kept my eyes closed, praying that when I opened them I'd be in the comfort of my own bedroom, that Joanna would be lying with her back to me, protecting her big bump. I prayed that what had happened the day before had simply been the most vivid of nightmares and I was now back in the real world.

I opened my eyes. The cream walls of Abby Suite 2 met my gaze. As I turned towards Joanna, I noticed that the nightie which had once been stretched over her bump sagged sadly. I pulled the duvet away and walked over to the refrigerated cot, on which the thermometer alternated between 9 and 10 degrees Celsius. *This* was now the real world.

The night before, there had been very little to tell Edith apart from a healthy baby. There was nothing eerie or strange about our daughter. She was a big girl, born five weeks prematurely on the 99th centile, looking like a normal newborn at full term. Perhaps this made the day of her birth a lot easier, resembling somehow the day of Josiah's birth two years before. But as I leaned over her cot to give her a kiss, the façade of normality began to crumble.

The smell of death now hung in the air. Her top layer of skin had begun to peel away from a dried-out, reddened underlayer. Unable to live on borrowed life and air from Joanna, she had deflated and now *looked* dead. I took her into my arms and her cheeks squished as I tried to keep her head upright, before resting it against my chest. While Joanna turned in bed, I stood next to the window with Edith in my arms, looking out towards the dreary brick wall. I had a sudden urge to take her out of this place – to go and show her the world, or just the sky even. If this was our last day together, surely we should go and do something?

Of course, I knew this wasn't possible, and that Edith was hardly missing out on seeing the world when she was in the presence of God. Sitting down on the couch with her on my lap, I thought about her in that perfect place, having similar thoughts about her parents. About how we were missing out, and how she'd love to show us around the place, where the sky is bluer, the sun brighter and where death is dead for ever. The door slowly creaked open and Mikaela popped her head in.

'Can I get you a tea or coffee?' she asked. 'Breakfast'll be on its way soon.'

'Could we have a coffee, please?' I said, turning to Joanna for her agreement.

'Yup,' Mikaela nodded. 'Milk, sugar?'

'Just a splash of milk for both of us,' Joanna replied, as Mikaela hurried off. There was something comforting in the exchange, a reminder of the everyday filling me with hope that maybe, one day, life could return to something of what we'd once known. Perhaps a morning coffee was our first step on the long journey towards recovery.

Two minutes later, Mikaela appeared again at the door, precariously holding it open with one foot while squeezing a coffee tray through.

'Here we are,' she said, removing her foot and letting the door close behind her. 'As I say, breakfast is on its way, so would you like me to do your bloods and injection now? Or shall we wait until after breakfast?'

Joanna looked confused.

'You were told about this, right?' Mikaela asked, rolling her eyes. Again, witnessing the usual annoyances of the workplace made me smile with its reminder of life outside these cream walls. 'Well, the bloods are for routine testing, and the injection is just to thin your blood – you know – because you're prone to clotting after a stillbirth.'

'That's OK,' Joanna said, smiling at Mikaela, who was still shaking her ponytail. 'I'll have them after breakfast, if that's all right?'

'Yup, that's fine. Also, I've been on the phone to the bereavement midwives who said they'll pop by a bit later. What are you planning to do today? Were you hoping to go home or stay for a bit longer? It's completely up to you . . . whatever you'd like.'

I'd just assumed that we'd go home that day but, aware of my tendency to rush through difficult things, I wanted to know what other parents in our situation tended to do.

'Everyone's different . . . Your milk's in this little jug,' Mikaela said, distracted as she transferred the coffee mugs to our bedside table. 'Some parents want to leave as soon as they can, but others want to spend as much time as possible with their baby.'

I looked to Joanna, not trusting my own preferences. 'I think we'll go home later today,' she replied. 'Jonny's parents are looking after our son, so they'll come and pick us up.'

Although this is what I would have chosen, it felt impossible. How could any parents, with any degree of love for their child, walk out of a room, never to see that precious girl again? How could we ever say goodbye to Edith? While the labour had previously been my biggest fear, I hadn't even considered what lay ahead in the coming hours.

Joanna

Distraction is often what allows us to cope with suffering. But when the coffee's been poured, the breakfast's eaten and the bloods are taken, there's little distraction to be found in a lightly furnished hospital room. It didn't take long before my thoughts wandered off to deeper things than whether to have tea or coffee. I looked at Edith and wondered how anyone who didn't believe in God could look at their stillborn child and ever find any hope. But then again, how could any Christian be in the same position without having any questions or doubts?

Since I was eight years old, I'd known a God who loves children. Jesus welcomed little ones into his arms, and said that to enter the kingdom of God we have to become like children. It was my relationship with this loving God that grew my love for babies made in his image – born, unborn or stillborn. And yet it was my relationship with this sovereign God that meant I had to face an uncomfortable truth that I couldn't get away from: *he had taken my little girl.*

Regardless of any future post-mortem, in a world where nothing happens outside God's control, the underlying reason why Edith wasn't breathing was because God had numbered her days at 247. But *why*? Why did he take her when she could have lived? Why us? Why her? The question 'Why?' would surely remain for the rest of our lives. But in the absence of answers to my questions, there were things I knew about God that came alive in Abby Suite 2, when everything else felt dead.

As I reached out to take Edith into my arms, my maternal instincts reminded me that God calls himself 'Father'. He could have described his relationship to us in any way, but he chose to call himself 'Daddy'. Sitting up in bed with her on my lap, unable to peel my eyes from her face, I felt some comfort knowing that the love I felt was not something God hadn't experienced. In fact, my love for Edith was only a pale reflection of the love that Father God has always had for his Son, Jesus. I'd always cherished that moment in the Garden of Gethsemane, when Jesus gives an insight into his relationship with his Father, at a time before anyone was born, unborn or stillborn:

> 'Father, I want those you have given me to be with me where I am, and to see my glory, the glory you have given me because you loved me before the creation of the world.'
> (John 17:24)

No, I didn't know why God had taken Edith. But I did know that he wanted me to experience the love and glory that Jesus had always enjoyed before he created the world. Not only that, I knew that Jesus himself wanted Edith to be where he is, to experience the love that God the Father, Son and Spirit have always shared and enjoyed. Maybe that's why he took her when he did. Perhaps a harder question to answer was: if he wanted me to be where he is, why was he taking so long to bring *me* home? Why delay?

But I didn't need more whys. I put my cup on the bedside table, Edith on the bed and slumped down next to her.

They say grief comes in waves. But during those hours, what washed over me was less seaside tides and more boiling kettles. It was as though something was stuck inside my body, with no escape. It beat against my chest and shot through my arms. It felt like pain, but it was love. It was a fierce tide of that divine emotion that Jesus was talking about. I was experiencing something of Father God's love for his own child but, unlike his happiness in his Son, my love would never be a cause for joy, only sadness. In this world, I would never express my love for her, chasing her from bath to bed; we'd never smile, seeing her hold up her achievement certificate at the end of term. My deep, deep maternal love was very much alive, but the object of my love was dead. So it felt like pain. And it felt unfair.

Jesus wanted me to be where both he and Edith were, and now so did I. I wanted to experience that glory – the glory of his love, that freedom from suffering. I wanted to be able to look Edith in the face and see her smile. I wanted to smile back. I wanted my love to feel like happiness, not pain. But I was here, in Abby Suite 2, with my trapped love, unable to move, unable to enjoy the love I had so much of. And while it felt unfair, I knew that it wasn't. What claim did I have against this God who's no stranger to having his own heart broken? While he'd created us to know and love and enjoy the glory that Jesus experienced before the creation of the world, we'd walked away from him. 'So the LORD was sorry he had ever made them and put them on the earth. It broke his heart' (Genesis 6:6, NLT).

Wouldn't it have been easier for God never to have created this world – this world of broken hearts and trapped loves? The Lord was 'sorry' he had ever made the people who rejected him, and who led this world into a path of devastation and death. Wouldn't it have been better if we'd never conceived Edith? For that egg to have remained unfertilized? As ever, the broken-hearted wish they'd never loved in the first place.

When God's children walked away from him, breaking his heart, I imagine he too experienced a trapped love – not because he needed us in order to be complete, but simply because he *loves* us, as we love Edith. It was this love that compelled him to pursue us, to send his only Son to bring us back. God's love drove him not only to experience the loss of a child, but to choose it. Jesus went willingly to the cross to take the punishment we deserved for turning our backs on God. In this way, the cross is the greatest symbol of God's love for his children. Only so vast a love would lead to such a sacrifice, and only justice for sin, sin so horrific to bring about a place like this world where babies die, would suffice. God would even turn his back on his Son.

At noon, darkness came over the whole land until three in the afternoon. And at three in the afternoon Jesus cried out in a loud voice, '*Eloi, Eloi, lema sabachthani?*' (which means 'My God, my God, why have you for-saken me?').
(Mark 8:33–34)

Stroking the skin-peels of my dead daughter, I wanted justice for her death, but I only had a God to blame who'd borne the justice I deserved in the dying body of his Son. I wanted to shake my fist at him, but looking back at me was a Father who himself had lost a child in order to make me, and my Edith, his own children. The 'whys' around Edith's death would surely continue, but for that moment they dried up when faced with a God who doesn't offer hope to grieving parents from a distance, but as one who has felt the same pain we were experiencing.

Jonny

I'd spent nearly twenty-four hours confined in the Abby Suite, so I needed to stretch my legs. I walked down a long corridor, past whispering midwives with clipboards. Pushing open double doors, I walked through triage, the emergency waiting room where all of this had begun. Anxious-looking women sat next to partners, holding their bumps, while others took cursory glances at repeats of *Homes Under the Hammer*. It felt strange to be living their worst nightmare. I was desperate to be in their shoes, still with the hope that the baby was just having a quiet day. I'd endured those same episodes of daytime TV on multiple hospital trips with both Jos and Edith . . . rubbing Joanna's back . . . asking if she'd felt anything yet. Three times we came back, our baby healthy, but one time we discovered the worst. Despite the worry on those parents' faces, I would have given anything to be in their position, with just one more throw of the dice.

I walked through the cafe, past the front desk and into the fresh air. Bright clouds dragged across a blue sky as cars were dropping off pregnant women. A middle-aged couple pulled up behind them, with a pink 'It's a girl!' helium balloon. Despite all the kind visits from friends and my fellow church leaders the evening before, nobody would be bringing our little girl a balloon today.

I crossed the busy road and reached the pavement which leads down to the university campus. It was late September – the time of year when the sun loses its strength and the shadows become longer. Freshers at the university flitted between stalls of different clubs and societies, picking up goody-bags and other campus paraphernalia along the way. I thought of myself at one such Freshers' Fair, twelve years before. Life was simpler then – full of opportunity and promise. I was heading out into the world, forging a life of my own, too young and naive to recognize that the same life which offers so much can leave you with so little.

I sat down on a bench where I could be lost in the crowd. How could any of these people know that my life had just been changed for ever? That in a matter of hours, I'd close the door on my own flesh and blood? Then again, what did I know of *their* lives? Crowds can't suffer. But crowds are made up of people who may look OK but who are formed out of their pain.

Sitting in front of the University of Birmingham Game of Thrones Society and overhearing exaggerated promises of the improvement in life quality for any prospective member, life had lost its joy for me. Despite the low sun's glare, the world felt dark – a cruel game of looking for ladders upwards to higher and better things, but where, at any turn, you could land on a snake, propelling you down to where you started. *What was the point?*

Two students came and sat on the bench next to me, opening their goody-bags, excited to see the new life that the Game of Thrones Society promised them. Unable to put up with what felt like pointless chat, I meandered back to the hospital. People with briefcases overtook me, clearly with things to do, clients to see and places to be. But I was in no rush; I climbed slowly up the hospital path, strolled past more excited grandparents, past the front desk, through triage, where a new cohort of anxious mums and dads now sat watching *Escape to the Country*, down the corridor of labour screams and back into Abby Suite 2, where I found both of my girls, sleeping.

One of them stirred when I came in, lifting a sleep-mask from her eyes.

'Are you OK? Where did you go?' Joanna asked, rubbing her eyes.

'I just went for a walk down to the university. All the freshers have arrived.'

Joanna put her head back on the pillow, replacing her sleep-mask.

'Shall I begin to pack up our stuff?' I asked. On the face of it, it was a pretty mundane question. But it hid the horrors of the inevitable – it was nearly time to leave Edith.

'Yeah, you can, but Mikaela's coming in a sec to do Edith's footprints and take some photographs. But let's get ready to go, and then we can spend some time with her.'

A few minutes later, Mikaela appeared, holding two sachets. Joanna lifted Edith out of her cot and angled her feet towards Mikaela, who opened the sachets, took out what looked like a baby wipe and skimmed the underside of Edith's left foot.

'Right, bring her foot towards the paper and I'll press it down,' she said, taking Edith's foot into her hands. She pressed and pulled it away from the paper, leaving a little grey footprint, before repeating the process with her right. 'How does that look? That's all right, isn't it?'

It was more than all right. Here was the unique footprint that God had designed for our little girl.

'And I've brought the camera to get some photos of her,' she said, pulling it from her pocket. 'Shall we put some of these toys in her cot?'

As well as the army of cuddly toys that the hospital gives bereaved parents, we had brought along a bear which Josiah had 'bought' for his sister. Edith slept as quietly as all of her toys while Mikaela took some photos.

'We're going to spend a few final minutes with her now, and then my dad's coming to pick us up,' I told Mikaela. The words seemed cold and heartless. Leaving our daughter in a room on her own, I felt like a neglectful dad, shunning my main responsibility to protect her. *Was this really happening?* It's the kind of thing you read about in books or see in films. We're not built to say a last goodbye to anyone, let alone our children who depend on us. But the truth was that she *didn't* depend on us and she was no longer in our care. I would always be her dad – but she was being looked after now by her heavenly Father.

We lined up our two bags next to the door, and Joanna picked Edith up out of her cot. Sitting down on the sofa, we looked at our lifeless daughter for a few moments before our strength gave way and we choked on tears. Passing her between us, we bit our lips, pawing at our cheeks, unable to get rid of the pent-up emotion of what we were about to do.

Running out of tears, I picked up my Bible, flicked to John 11 and began to read the chapter from beginning to end. This Jesus smelt the death of Lazarus, as we smelt the death of our daughter. He wept, as we wept. Would he raise our little girl from the dead, just as he raised Lazarus? I prayed one last time, but her eyes remained closed and her tongue silent.

'Are you ready?' I asked Joanna. How can anyone ever be ready? The only way to leave that room was to numb the pain and act in defiance of it. To go against every parental inclination, we simply had to walk. I placed Edith in her cot, kissing her nose, as a tear fell from my face and splashed her forehead. I held her hand for three last precious seconds. Like desperate homeowners trying to gather as many prized possessions into a case while their house was burning down, we were trying our best to absorb as much of her as we could possibly hold on to.

'Goodbye, little one – see you soon,' I choked. We turned and we walked, opening the door to a future we never wanted, before closing the door to the one we longed to have back. Walking into the corridor, I felt the weight of gravity for the first time. Unable to know what to do with such agonizing, trapped turmoil, my legs simply buckled and I fell to the ground, pounding the wall with piercing shrieks. I felt like I was dying, and in a way I was. Jesus had promised that following a crucified Saviour to his heavenly kingdom would feel like death. And here I was, on the hospital floor, grounded beneath the burden of the cross that Jesus had carried before us – the one he'd called us to carry too.

A midwife, unaware of our situation, ushered us into the Family Room, where Mikaela soon came to comfort us. We'd done the hardest bit; the door was closed. Now, we just had to walk out of the hospital.

Walking up that corridor for the last time felt like walking up the Calvary Road behind our Lord Jesus. He did it 'for the joy that was set before him' (Hebrews 12:2). That joy is the same joy which our Edith is currently experiencing and which we long for, far more now than ever before.

We didn't walk out on our little girl. We merely handed her over to the perfect Father, of whom I was only ever going to be a faint reflection. And he will keep her safe in his everlasting arms, until we meet again.

Interlude: the voice

When they arrived in Bethany, a crowd had gathered: women on their knees, scooping handfuls of dust from the ground, weeping, wincing, with worn expressions, looking upwards. Men knelt prostrate, palms straight out on the dirt. A collective cry reverberated between the olive trees and the rocks, while crows circled overhead. Jesus breathed deeply and walked between the mourners.

Suddenly Martha came rushing up and flung her arms around him, as she too dropped to her knees, tear-drenched hair sticking to her face. She looked up at Jesus, confused:

'Lord, if only you'd come sooner. *If only you'd been here* . . . Lord, he wouldn't have died. Lord, he wouldn't have – I sent for you, Lord . . .' Her words dried up.

Jesus looked into her bloodshot eyes. '*Martha*' – even the way he said her name soothed some of the sorrow – 'Martha . . . your brother will rise,' he said, wiping her tears with his index finger.

'I know, Lord. We will see him again at the resurrection of the dead, at the last day.' But Jesus' expression became sterner – *safer*, even.

'I *am* the resurrection and the life. Anyone who believes in me will live, despite dying. Anyone who believes in me will never die. Do you understand, Martha? Do you believe this?' he said, holding her arms intently.

'I do, Lord,' replied Martha, holding back more tears. 'You are the Messiah. You are the Son of God.' She took a step back. 'I need to get Mary. Don't go anywhere,' she whispered, turning on her heel. Jesus turned to his disciples, most of whom avoided his gaze, huddled together like awkward adolescents lost in an adult world. James drew lines in the gravel with the sole of his sandal.

'Do you still not understand?' Jesus called out to the Twelve. But they didn't know how to answer.

Mary came rushing, a crowd of mourners behind her. Stopping in front of Jesus to catch her breath, she fell at his feet. 'Where have you been?' She arched her neck upwards, straining her eyes against the sun. 'You could have saved him . . .'

Jesus saw their grief and was cut to the heart. The pain in his friends' eyes he felt in his hands; their tears were now becoming his own. *This world!* he bristled. *Look what it has become! A wasteland of death and decay! Oh, the horror of sin that it should bring such grief.* But Jesus spoke calmly.

'Where is he buried?'

Mary and Martha led Jesus away, while his disciples joined the mourners from behind. The midday heat merged with the sultry swell of the crowd. Jesus breathed in warm dust. The branches above him swirled in the hot breeze. He pictured his Father's world as the crowd carried him along – how he longed to be back there where death had died, where his children would be healed and where their cries would be met only with the divine voice of the One who used pain to bring them to himself . . . His work here wasn't finished.

'It's that one, Lord,' said Mary, pointing Jesus towards a large stone, two or three times bigger than himself. The crowd stopped and Jesus stepped towards the stone. Onlookers watched from behind as Jesus paused, sweat dripping from his beard. He stared at the tomb, like a statue carved into the rock. Muted muttering gave way to silence. They waited. But Jesus didn't move, his gaze fixed ahead of him.

Jesus thought of the evenings spent around Lazarus's table – laughing and joking over bread and wine. He could see his face – *oh, the life in that face!* His smile and love for his sisters. And now, here he was, dead. Feeling the pointed gaze of the crowd from behind, his hands began to shake with the grief and the anger that rose up within him. He bit his bottom lip and closed his eyes. Looking up to the cloudless sky, his knees gave way to gravity's grasp and, letting out a loud groan, Jesus fell to the dust. The crowd stood still.

'You see how much he loved him,' Mary whispered, breathing out deeply and shaking her head. The man in front turned, weeping and weary. 'Yes – but couldn't this man who opened blind eyes have kept Lazarus from dying?' Mary didn't answer at first, looking instead at Jesus, who was slowly getting to his feet and moving towards the tomb.

'Don't you fear God?' Mary managed. 'Don't you believe in the resurrection of the dead? Jesus is the resurrection – he'll raise Lazarus up in his kingdom. The Master knows what he's doing.'

'Get rid of the stone,' Jesus shouted. The crowd whispered and Martha stepped forward.

'But Lord . . .' she stopped and looked into Jesus' eyes, hesitating. 'He's been dead for four days . . . It'll smell.'

Jesus turned and faced Martha, the crowd and his disciples. Nodding his head, he said, 'Didn't I tell you, Martha, if you believe in me, you will see the glory of God?'

His voice held an authority that could have told the sun to drop out of the sky or the ground to be upended. His hands commanded a power that could have picked up the stone and thrown it away. But as two men struggled with it, Jesus looked up and spoke.

'Father, I thank you that you have heard me. I know that you always hear me, but I said this for the benefit of the people standing here, so that they'd believe that you sent me – so that they'd believe that in me there is life – life beyond this darkened world, on the other side of grief. Oh, Father, that they'd know that I am the resurrection and the life, that they'd glorify your name in life and death, and be brought safely home. Father, I do this for the benefit of the people standing here.'

Jesus stared down the tomb with eyes of fire. The stench of death filled the air. But with the voice that spoke stars into space, Jesus roared, 'Lazarus, come out!'

Amid gasps of horror, the dead man, covered in linen, stumbled out of the darkness and into the light, pulling at the cloth around his face. Resolutely, Jesus turned to the astonished crowd and, walking off, simply said, 'Take off the grave clothes and let him go.'

Mary and Martha followed Jesus, while the crowd laughed with joy or cried.

'Your brother will die again,' Jesus said, turning towards his friends. They looked into his eyes and saw something they'd never previously seen. 'Believe in me,' Jesus said, 'and though you'll die, you *will* live. Do you believe?'

4

Too short a grave

Jonny

We'd made tomato and basil soup for all the family. Like Martha, I scurried around clearing up teacups and bowls. People apologized for interrupting conversations as they rescued nieces and nephews from a tumble – or chunks of bread from the carpet. It could have been Christmas, or Josiah's second birthday, if it hadn't been for the fact that we were all wearing black.

The doorbell rang and I opened the door to my parents. Dad stepped towards me and squeezed me with those same arms that had picked me up when I'd fallen over as a toddler. Though today the hug felt stronger, as if it was just as much for him as for me.

'You...' He stopped, struggling already to hold back the tears. He shook his head, gave up on the words and hugged me again. Joanna appeared from the lounge, wearing a long, black dress patterned with light feathers from neck to ankle.

'You look lovely, darling,' said Mum, putting down what looked like enough food to keep us going for months. 'And where's that little boy?'

On cue, Josiah came careering around the corner, digger in hand, and gave his grandparents a hug. Apart from his smart clothes, this was just another day for a nearly-two-year-old.

For us, though, his innocent antics were a tonic, keeping us holding on to life's joys, which, as we know, so often share the same soil as its sorrows.

Conversation grew quieter as I busied myself – more cups, more bowls, 'Have you had enough soup?' – more toys to clear and dishes to wash. Putting a handful of crockery down on the kitchen surface, I choked on a breath before inhaling the next. Nobody saw, but everyone knew all too well that I wasn't coping with this. Outwardly I was OK but inwardly I was scared – scared of seeing Edith's tiny coffin, scared of being so close to that little girl who I'd said goodbye to three weeks earlier, and scared about how I might respond. What would I do? Could I really be trusted not to lift the lid to see her one last time? What would she look like now? Had the post-mortem surgeons left scars from examining her organs, her brain? Had they been careful with the stitching? Did they remember to put in the cuddly toys that we'd bought her? Was she warm enough?

While others put kids down for naps and brushed their teeth, I didn't feel I could move from the kitchen, as though my busyness had arrived at a sudden natural end. I'd come to put the spoons in the dishwasher but they remained on the side, immovable lumps of steel that would stay there for ever as soap suds fizzed in the sink.

'Jonny, she's here.' I looked out of the kitchen window and there it was – something so very real, yet something so out of this world, that I couldn't help but stare. Like a little girl trying on but barely filling her mum's high heels, Edith's little box swam in space inside the oversized hearse. Her new home was a beautiful white, tastefully draped with sage leaves and ivory flowers. And yet it was grotesquely shocking.

In those brief moments, however, what shocked me most was that, despite all the funeral planning, I'd never stopped to think that we'd have her *here* with us, outside our front door. The door through which we'd brought Josiah home, wrapped up tight in his winter clothes, warm and snug in his car seat. And now she too had come home to be with us, wrapped tightly in her burial clothes, warm and snug – I hoped – in a coffin.

Like the father of the prodigal son in a very different scenario, I wasted no time but went straight to the door, opened it and went out in my socks to welcome her home. As the undertakers got out of the hearse they stood dutifully next to it, while I stood stupidly on the damp pavement, unable to remember what exactly I'd come out to do. I just looked, knowing that this first sight, which lasted only a few seconds, would stay with me for ever. A few spots of rain landed on my suit jacket, and I turned around and simply walked back into the house.

We followed the hearse in convoy to the church, where our friends and more family were waiting for us. I'd only attended a handful of funerals before Edith's, but this was the first one I'd been to where the coffin would be carried by only one pallbearer.

Getting out of the car, my parents gave me the same look they'd often given me as a teenager.

'Are you sure you can do this, Jonny?' Mum asked. 'If you've changed your mind, the undertaker said he'd be very happy to carry her in.'

'I'm OK, Mum – I want to do it,' I replied, moving towards the back of the hearse where the undertakers were holding

Edith's coffin. I put my arms out as instructed, as if I were holding a large tray, and they placed her across my arms. Her weight pressed against my skin lightly – the body that God had stitched together was real, weighty even.

Joanna, Mum and Dad went off to find their seats at the front of church, while I stayed behind in the atrium, waiting for Arvo Pärt's *Spiegel im Spiegel* to begin. Before the minor chords and violins sounded, it was just me and her. I'd never been on my own with my little girl before. And here we were, about to walk down a church aisle. Except that this wasn't how it was meant to go. Walking her down the aisle wasn't meant for now. In my mind, she'd always be dressed in white, a bouquet of flowers in her hands. Her auburn hair would be flowing, her figure feminine. Standing outside the church door, waiting to go in, she'd kiss her old man's cheek and say, 'You ready, Daddy?' And we'd walk slowly down the aisle, arm in arm. Her high heels would softly click on the stone floor, while heads would turn slowly, smiling.

It wasn't meant to be like this.

The minor chords began and the doors opened in front of me. I began to walk but it was only the sound of my heels that could be heard. My daughter wasn't in a white dress but in a white box. No heads turned, and there were no smiles.

Joanna

After the funeral, we followed the hearse slowly towards the cemetery. We didn't know how many would come, but when we pulled in and made our way towards Section 13 it was as if the whole church had arrived. My dad was there, dog-collar on, ready to lead the burial service.

I walked towards the gaping hole in the ground, around which stood friends and family, and a pile of mud. Looking at your daughter's grave is like looking at an enemy that is about to swallow your hope whole. It was so badly out of proportion; it seemed to keep going and going and going downwards, further and further into the ground, and yet it was so strangely short.

'On the back of your service sheets, you'll find our final hymn: "We rest on Thee".' I'd heard my dad lead church services all my life, his voice as familiar as any. And yet, gathered around a tiny grave in south Birmingham, with Mum a few hundred miles away in a hospice bed, this was a whole new world. And still God remained, and remains, the same.

We rest on Thee, our Shield and our Defender;
We go not forth alone against the foe;
Strong in Thy strength, safe in Thy keeping tender.
We rest on Thee, and in Thy Name we go.[4]

Fifty voices, singing unaccompanied about our God and his power to preserve us beyond death, raised a collective fist against the unnumbered graves around us – trophies of death and Satan – that stood neatly in row after row.

Then Jonny and his dad stood either side of that deep and short hole before lowering Edith into the ground, the pile of mud next to them clashing violently with their clean suits and the whiteness of the coffin. Once she had finally found her resting place, six feet underground, someone handed a small wooden box of mud across to me. I took a handful of the dirt and let it slip out of my fingers, down, down, until it spread over the pristine white and silver handles of the coffin. After passing the box to Jonny, I looked at my hands and the dirt congregating in the fault-lines of my right palm – a reminder that the dirt of death belonged to me, and that one day it would be me being lowered in that box, to lie under six-feet worth of mud.

From mud you came and to mud you shall return. The promise was clear, and my grubby palms were just the trailer of death's hold over us all. It wouldn't spare my mum, or me. It wouldn't even spare my baby, or anyone else's baby. No, next to Edith was Daniel. Next to him, Kayleigh. Next to her, Brody. And next to him, Amber – 'Born asleep', their headstones read.

Jonny

As the October breeze picked up fallen leaves and threw them around our feet, the two of us stood arm in arm. Peering into the bowels of the earth that had just swallowed the body of our daughter, I felt angry at the world. *Such a wasteland of death and decay and dirt!* It felt as though we'd said to Jesus, 'Lord, the one you love is sick – *dead*, even.' And yet he hadn't come. Or like those in the crowd, we were thinking, 'If he can raise Lazarus from the dead, couldn't Jesus have kept this little girl from dying?' We were like Mary and Martha: 'Jesus, why didn't you act sooner to save our little one?'

We couldn't escape the fact that Jesus had never made things right immediately. He hadn't prevented the death of Lazarus, but rather he delayed coming and went to stand next to his grave. Just as he stood with Mary and Martha, he stood with us next to Edith's grave, offering us the same promise:

'I am the resurrection and the life. The one who believes in me will live, even though they die.' While we had very few answers, this much was sure: Jesus had always allowed the grief of death to roll over his followers before reuniting them with their loved ones. And so too, Jesus was there with us, allowing the sting of death to hurt, before we'd be reunited with her, and with him in his kingdom.

We wanted Jesus to snap his fingers and make it all right now. But his delay in raising Lazarus was no spiritual anomaly. God's victory over sin, death and hell at the cross didn't transport his followers into an instant resurrection. On that first Good Friday, Jesus wasn't raised victoriously the moment he died. No – between Good Friday and Easter Sunday there was Saturday, when the Light of the World had been extinguished, the Bread of Heaven had been left to spoil, and the Resurrection and the Life lay lifeless, left to decay. Jesus' broken and bruised body was taken down from the cross and buried, like Edith, in a dirty grave. He identified with all of us with dirt on our hands, under God's curse of death.

For years, Joanna and I had clung fast to the promise of forgiveness of sins, won for us on Good Friday. We'd praised God for the promise of resurrection life, achieved for us on the first Easter Sunday. And yet, standing next to Edith's grave, it was that gloomy Saturday in between that brought us most comfort. We were stuck in the middle of being saved from this world of sin, death and grief and being brought into the place where our tears would be wiped dry. Lazarus was no outlier; the resurrection that Jesus brings always comes after delay. His followers must always wait patiently.

As long as we would mourn Edith's death, sit around the dinner table with one of our children missing, look at family photographs with one of us not there, live on this side of heaven – it *would* be Saturday. Jesus would allow this day to continue with the promise that, while death's dirt will surely cover us in burial, all who believe in him will be raised. Jesus' resurrection is the promise that our Saturday's dusk will give way to Sunday's dawn, his voice will be heard, and we will go to be with him and with those whom we have lost in Jesus.

While the October sun cast long shadows over Edith's grave, the question Jesus asked us was the same one he asked Martha in her grief: 'Do you believe this?' (John 11:26).

Did I believe that Jesus was the resurrection and the life? Did I believe that while it looked like death had had the final word, Jesus had conquered death? Did I believe that while there is no sure hope in this world, Jesus was our hope of a renewed world? Did I believe that my daughter had died so that God's Son might be glorified through it? Did I believe that things weren't as they seemed? Did I believe that, while everything pointed to Edith being dead, she was now more alive than I was? Did I believe that Jesus was the resurrection and the life, and that while he died for me he was now alive, waiting to bring me home? *Did I believe this?*

Taking Joanna's arm, we walked slowly towards the cemetery gate. Our shadows spilled over rows of graves. More clearly than ever, I realized that death – even the death of our daughter – should never be the reason to doubt the gospel. Defeating death, once and for all, was the very reason that Jesus had lived and died. In that cemetery we were as close to understanding the heart of the good news as we'd ever been, and likely ever will be. As we walked past grave after grave, it was as if I were walking alongside the Saviour – the only One who had defeated the grave – and hearing Jesus ask me the same question that he asked his disciples after many had deserted him: 'You don't want to leave too, do you?' (John 6:67).

Jesus alone is the antidote to death and decay. So my response could only echo Simon Peter's: 'Lord, to whom shall we go? You have the words of eternal life' (John 6:68).

We walked on, not knowing what the future might bring.

PART 1: WEEPING

PART 2: WALKING

PART 3: WAITING

Excerpt from Joanna's diary

28 October 2018

The boys are out. I'm meant to be processing and writing, but I don't really know how to. I don't really know what I feel or think. All that comes to mind is: my daughter has died, my mum has died.

When the boys left earlier, I wanted to go with them, but I couldn't motivate myself to get dressed and out of the house. I can barely motivate myself to respond to people asking me how I'm doing. When they left the house, I thought maybe I'd leave too. Maybe I'd just go somewhere. Get out of the house, have coffee. Feel the cold and the wind and the outside elements. Or, I thought, maybe I would leave and go and see Mum and Edith. I'd rather be there than in this bed. I'd be free from guilt, free from fear. No one can die there.

But I could never do that to Jonny, or Jossy – or anyone who has experienced our loss. I'd only be adding to that. So I'll probably just stay here, unsure how to process things, or respond, or write. 'Help me, Father,' is about all I can manage today.

5

Blame and shame

Joanna

Thursday 1 November felt like a new beginning, and not only because it was my birthday. Sitting with my feet up on the dashboard, I reached into my McDonald's bag for another handful of chips, while Jonny filled up the car with petrol for the journey home. Josiah had fallen asleep in the back.

In twenty-nine years, I'd never experienced anything like what had happened over the previous weeks. Death. Birth. Funeral. Followed now by the death and funeral of my mum. The day before, I'd seen Jonny and my two brothers carry her into church on their shoulders – something that should have felt like an out-of-body experience, but by now it felt perversely normal. It was hard to remember our previous life – the excitement of looking forward to a family day out, relaxing on a Saturday evening, the stability and structure of life's routines. In one sense we were driving back to this previous life, but we knew it would never be the same again. At best, it would only be a new phase of grief.

Jonny had organized a small gathering of friends for the afternoon, to mark my birthday. It was always going to be a muted affair, but there was something comforting about sitting and chatting with friends over a plate of party food, as though I'd entered a photograph from happier days gone by.

Josiah was running around with his dinosaur, Jonny was doing the drinks round, and the Wi-Fi signal kept interrupting the playlist. Despite all the caveats, we'd finally come home to begin rebuilding our shattered lives.

The funeral planning and family visits had protected us from the onslaught of emotions and questions. We powered through it all on adrenaline, making decisions about orders of service and flower arrangements. But when the funeral was over and there were no more to-do lists, the waves of grief rolled in and broke around me, sometimes feeling as though they were hauling me under and holding my head beneath the water. Surrounded by so much death, I was desperate to keep our indoor field of flowers alive, but eventually they also died. Before long, the only evidence in our house that we'd lost our baby girl was the pile of gifted chocolate in the kitchen cupboard – and the second cot in Josiah's bedroom, lying empty.

Days at home often felt aimless. Waking up each morning didn't signal the beginning of any kind of routine. While having space simply to lie in bed was exactly what I needed, the sounds of a silent house provided fertile soil for painful shoots of guilt to take root. Feeling pinned to the bed under an immovable burden of grief, question after question weighed in with fresh accusations, finding any possible way to point the finger at me for what had happened to Edith.

Why are you on maternity leave? Can you even call yourself a new mum? Mums protect their children. You could have stopped this. What if you'd eaten more healthily? What if you hadn't had a bath the night she died? Was it because you'd spent eight months carrying Jos about, or sitting cooped up in the car, on the way to and from Sheffield to see your mum? You were stressed and busy – that's why she died.

I couldn't shake off the belief that somehow this was my fault, that it was my body that had let her down and had let her die. I'd failed in my one responsibility as a mum of an unborn child.

Even when I wasn't keeping pace, life marched on, demanding that I be OK. Jonny had to go back to work and Josiah's needs didn't stop. There were days when I'd wake up and couldn't even open my eyes for the darkness all around me, but I still had to get up and entertain a nearly-two-year old. *Can't you just be happy that you've got him? Don't you know that some mums have no children in the house at all?* The accusations continued, but the space to process any kind of answer was getting squeezed.

While time on my own had led to feelings of blame, being forced out of the house led to feelings of shame. It meant facing the possibility of being asked the kind of question that, mercifully, I was asked only once.

'So, how's life with two?' she smiled enthusiastically, heavily pregnant herself and looking for advice. She hadn't heard, and I felt ashamed that I couldn't give her an answer. I didn't know what life was like with two – how I wished I did! The guilt flared up, as though I *should* know the answer, as if there *should* be two kids here, were it not for my reckless actions or lax attitude. I was to blame for this situation, and being in public meant I grew vulnerable and self-conscious, being without the baby that everyone had seen growing in my womb.

Going to the supermarket or getting my hair cut became fear-inducing activities. What if that shop assistant was working, that one who always asked how I was getting on in pregnancy? Was it Katie or Nadim who cut my hair the last time before Edith died? Would whoever it was mention the fact that I was there without either a bump or a baby? Or would they awkwardly pretend they hadn't noticed, consigning Edith's life to nothing more than an expired conversation-starter? Or worse: as my body slowly recovered, what if someone asked when I was due? It was the stuff of nightmares . . . sometimes literally.

It felt like salt in the wound that I was expected to carry on with life as normal. I felt fat and sore – the scars of labour that you can put up with while holding your newborn baby in your arms. Not to mention the hormones that tricked my body into thinking I actually had a newborn to look after. *Where had I left her? What had I done?* Edith's cot remained empty next to her brother's, except for some consolatory cuddly toys. My arms were empty too, my tummy flabby, and I was ashamed of myself – shame that was the poisoned fruit of a deep-seated conviction that I was to blame.

I felt fearful about the post-mortem. I felt like I would finally be found out for what I'd done, or not done, to bring about Edith's death. The jury's verdict would be in and my condemnation would be confirmed. But when the day arrived, it felt strangely comforting to walk through the doors of Birmingham Women's Hospital again, past reception and past triage, with daytime TV still beaming down to anxious women. This place felt like Edith's place – the place we'd met her, and loved her, and bathed her, and changed her, and *knew* her. That familiar smell and artificial warmth, the flurry of midwives, family visitors carrying tiny knitted garments, and doctors grabbing a meal deal from the volunteer-led coffee shop – this wasn't a place of nightmares but a safe space, where we could remember her, talk about her and bump into people who remembered what she looked like. After all, who could forget those sassy lips?

We went upstairs to the bereavement midwives' office and took a seat in the Quiet Room. Alison – who had held Edith, and my hand in the few counselling sessions since – offered us a coffee and assured us that Mr Parsons, the consultant, was on his way to explain the results. When she brought the coffee through, it was hard knowing that Alison was aware of the results. *Couldn't she tell us without Mr Parsons? Was her warm smile a show of empathy for what we were about to hear?*

About five minutes later, Mr Parsons came in, clutching a clipboard and a plastic file filled with paper. He apologized for being late, explaining that he'd been called urgently to the High Dependency Unit – a reminder that we were simply a drop in the ocean of anxious and grieving parents, not just in the Women's Hospital but in hospitals all round the country and all round the world. He sat down in front of us and took his pen out of his shirt pocket.

'First of all, I want to say that I'm so sorry for your loss,' he said, with a deep, West Midlands accent. 'In times like these, parents obviously want to know what happened to their baby, and so do we. The more we know, the more babies we can keep safe.' I began to guess what kind of news he was setting up with this preamble.

'Sometimes we can give parents a good idea of what we believe happened, and sometimes the results can be quite disappointing, not really providing any conclusive evidence.' Finishing his sentence, he opened the file and spread out a number of A4 sheets of paper in front of him. 'In your case, I'm afraid, there was no obvious cause behind Edith's death.'

Had I heard him correctly? If I had, there was nothing to be sorry for . . .

'The good news, however, is that there was nothing wrong with your placenta, or you – the post-mortem showed a completely healthy baby.'

It was perhaps only then, some months after Edith died, that a sense of relief broke through the burden of guilt that I'd been carrying on my shoulders. Of course, it was confusing that Edith appeared to be perfectly healthy but, walking back down the hospital corridor towards the main entrance, I allowed myself for the first time to believe what everyone else had been telling me since we'd lost our little girl. Edith didn't die as a result of a lack of love or care for her on my part. We were both perfectly healthy. And even if she had died because of a deficiency in my blood flow, or the strength of my placenta, or an infection that I'd caught, or if I'd simply got to the hospital too late, Edith died because God made the decision to bring her home – a decision I had no say in.

Jonny

Getting back to some kind of 'normal' exposed what we'd lost. Seeing families in the park, hearing that distinctive newborn cry, or simply looking into Josiah's – and Edith's – recently decorated bedroom, she was everywhere. We saw where she would have been, but was not. The question 'Why?' morphed more into 'Why us?' That question would have felt easier if we hadn't been Christians. We could put it down to a cruel twist of fate, a biological accident or a freak of nature. But I'd come to know and love a God who promised that no suffering was an accident, and that 'in all things God works for the good of those who love him' (Romans 8:28). Before losing Edith I believed this: not that those things were necessarily good in themselves, obviously, but I believed that the purpose of suffering in our lives as Christians was to make us more like Jesus – and this was a good thing.

But while I could assure Joanna that she, or her body, wasn't to blame for Edith's death, I too felt a similar, albeit spiritual, accusation of blame. Going for a walk after Joanna and Josiah had gone to bed, under a clear, cold December sky, I sat on a park bench and began to reason, *If God brings about suffering to make us more like Jesus, what if I'd been more like Jesus to start with? What if I'd pursued maturity more wholeheartedly? Then God wouldn't have had to take our daughter from us to achieve his purpose . . .*

While I knew that God wasn't punishing us, seeing other families who hadn't experienced baby loss, both at church and outside it, I wondered, *Are we more in need of God's work in our lives than them? Are we less like Jesus?* In some twist of the truth, I blamed myself for not being more spiritually mature, so that God was forced to do something so drastic to get through to me. Perhaps this was the Christian version of looking to a post-mortem to get answers, and so feel some semblance of control in what was otherwise a haze of confusion. Perhaps, if we could just blame ourselves – Joanna, physically, and me, spiritually – then at least we had *some* explanation for Edith's death, albeit one that piled guilt on top of raw grief.

Feeling a false sense of guilt didn't mean that I was innocent. My life obviously fell woefully short of God's perfection. But it felt that a healthy sense of conviction couldn't easily be disentangled from the false sense of guilt I felt around Edith's death. I just felt guilty. So I was forced to remember that Jesus' death covered all of my guilt; I didn't have to play a silly game of separating the true guilt of sin from the false guilt I felt for Edith's death. God wasn't weighing my godliness against my ungodliness, seeing if I would come out on the right side of some spiritual standard. Jesus died to take away all guilt and clothe me with his perfect righteousness, so God now related to me and Joanna as children, loved in the same way as his eternal Son.

What loving parent looks to catch his children out? 'You weren't praying enough for the health of your daughter . . . you didn't give her enough attention, so now you're going to pay the price.' My view of God had him looking down and saying coldly, 'You're not good enough – you hardly resemble Jesus at all, and to sort you out, I'm going to take away your daughter.' But this isn't the loving God of the cross.

The God of the cross demonstrated his love for us by the lengths of suffering he himself went to in Jesus. Through his work, he now relates to us, not as the guilty sinners we were, but as innocent saints and children who he delights in. Of course, this Father's love will mean discipline and correction at times in our lives. But to point the finger at ourselves for Edith's death didn't come from the design of God; it was a scheme of Satan, who never wastes any opportunity to accuse God's people of the guilt and shame that Jesus came to put away.

Joanna

I knew what many of our friends were quick to remind us, that God uses our suffering for his good purposes, as in the verse in Romans 8 above. But at times, if I'm honest, I felt a pressure to be able to explain exactly how God had used Edith's death to make me more like him. When getting out of bed felt like an achievement, taking steps forward in godliness felt like an impossibility. It felt as though others wanted to remind us of the Christian growth that God would bring, as a way to give some meaning to the suffering and maybe even to defend God's goodness. But some days it felt like there could be no purpose whatsoever in this darkness.

One Bible passage that I went back to time and time again was the beginning of the book of James. I found that, while we'll never fully understand God's purpose in our suffering this side of heaven, James gives a slightly different, and more encouraging, reason for why Edith died:

> Consider it pure joy, my brothers and sisters, whenever you face trials of many kinds, because you know that the testing of your faith produces perseverance. Let perseverance finish its work so that you may be mature and complete, not lacking anything.
> (James 1:2–4)

While the post-mortem showed no cause of death, this was the most encouraging answer as to why Edith died: God was, and is, producing *perseverance* in us. The way that God keeps us keeping on – the way he keeps us walking towards the heavenly city where children will no longer die – is through trials. Without trials, we'd wander from the path.

Lying in my bed, barely able to move, hearing that God's purpose in my suffering was first and foremost to bring about my maturity felt condemning. I felt like I'd gone backwards! And if so, maybe God *wasn't* at work in this. But if God's purpose in my suffering was perseverance I felt encouraged, because I was still there, clinging on to him. Even if all I could manage was: 'Help me, Father,' he was still my Father. Jesus was still Lord. Holding on to him in absolute brokenness was a better picture of the Christian life than when I was able to rely on my own strength. In my weakness, here was a reason I could point to for God bringing this trial into my life. I could say, 'Look, I'm still here, still a Christian, still plodding on, still clinging to Jesus in my desperate need.'

James is clear that when perseverance finishes its work, God will bring about a maturity and a completeness. This might be in a year's time – or in twenty years' time. But, for now, I know God is at work, simply because I'm still in the race. I'm still plodding on. And knowing how prone I am to wander from him, this could only be the good purpose of a loving Father, who never lets his children go. Ever.

6

Crying in community

Joanna

One of the hardest things to accept when you've lost a baby is that neither you nor others will truly know who that person was. For most, even knowing whether the baby was a boy or a girl remains a mystery. I felt devastated that I would know so little about Edith, that I'd be left guessing what her personality would be like, or what she would get into, or the woman she would grow up to be. The night before giving birth, I had an overwhelming desire to share Edith with others in the small amount of time we'd have to spend with her, just as any new mum proudly wants to present a newborn to friends and family. We ummed and aahed about it, but the night before giving birth I sat on our bed while Jonny spoke on the phone to his friend.

'Toby, we really don't want you to feel any pressure, but we'd love you to meet our little one. I know that might sound weird, but –' Jonny stopped mid-sentence and I heard Toby's voice jump in. Jonny was pacing up and down at the bottom of the bed before stopping to rest his foot against the skirting board. He was nodding his head, suppressing a smile.

'OK, mate,' he continued, 'we really appreciate that, but please tell Kath that, if she feels weird about it in any way, you guys don't have to come – we don't want you to feel any kind of pressure.'

Even after putting the phone down, we still felt unsure if we were placing too heavy a burden on our friends. Was it selfish to ask them to come, in order to satisfy our urge to share her? Was it fair to ask them to hold a dead baby, when we ourselves felt nervous about it?

The next evening, hours after giving birth, eight of us were squeezed between a hospital bed and a sofa in Abby Suite 2, passing Edith between ourselves. Before they arrived, I didn't know if I could keep it together, but before long it became obvious that I didn't have to.

As we told them the story of Edith's birth, our friends were weeping while looking lovingly into the closed eyes of the most peaceful newborn they'd ever held. We cried too, seeing their love for us, but also their love for her. Together we spoke about all the ways that Edith looked like her big brother, about whose nose she had and, of course, about where those sassy lips came from. In some mysterious way, the tears of those dear brothers and sisters in Christ dried some of our own. It was as if the weight of our pain was stored up in tears, and they'd relieved us of some of that burden. They'd cried some of them for us, and carried some of the grief on our behalf. They too were grieving the loss of a child they loved, and this time of shared grief was the very comfort of Christ, wrapping his arms around his weeping children.

For me, their comfort didn't translate into an immediate desire to go to church on the Sunday after saying goodbye to Edith. There are very few places in the world where babies seem to outnumber adults, but church feels like one of them. Leaving the house was hard enough, but leaving it to spend a few hours seeing so many little ones running around felt nearly impossible. If going out for coffee had felt too hard, I simply wouldn't have gone, without thinking too much more about it. But church was different.

I knew I didn't *have* to go. And in the shock of trauma, staying at home for a few weeks would have been totally understandable. But God's Word was, and is, food for our soul. If I missed a Sunday at the best of times I'd go hungry that week, but these weren't the best of times. This was famine, and my soul felt starved, crying out for the nourishment that only Jesus gives us in the gospel. I knew I needed it, but needing something isn't the same as wanting it and I really didn't want to go.

After some deliberation, we decided we would go, but we'd turn up late so we could sit at the back and leave if we needed to. I felt nervous walking up to the Youth Centre where our church meets, holding Jonny's arm while he pushed Josiah in the pushchair. Arriving ten minutes into the service, we found some seats at the back, trying to slip in without too much commotion. Once settled, we looked around and saw our church family, some with their heads in their hands, many with bleary eyes and blotched faces. I could hear crying from different parts of the room and see tissues strewn across the small tables. Jonny's co-leader – also Jonny – was at the front, leading our little church family through a service of lament. He preached on the Bible passage that had become so precious to us – Jesus standing by Lazarus's grave, weeping. Other brothers and sisters prayed to God for us, and for the church. Hearing their shaky voices, cries of confusion and over-whelming sadness brought back the comfort we'd felt with those close friends on the evening of Edith's birth. Jonny and I weren't the only ones grieving: letting others in allowed them to grieve and us to receive God's comfort. Being part of God's household meant that we shared our grief, felt our pain collectively, and we all sorely missed our daughter together. Here was the church *being* the church, the body of Christ working as God designed it.

Jonny

Having been involved in starting and leading a small church from scratch, I was already familiar with the Bible's description of the church being Christ's body and this had become dear to me:

> Just as a body, though one, has many parts, but all its many parts form one body, so it is with Christ. For we were all baptized by one Spirit so as to form one body – whether Jews or Gentiles, slave or free – and we were all given the one Spirit to drink . . . Now you are the body of Christ, and each one of you is a part of it.
> (1 Corinthians 12:12–13, 27)

For me, the picture of a diverse, yet unified, body had always captured something beautiful about the church – each body part, each person, using God-given gifts to serve the mission of seeing Jesus formed in people. We'd seen and celebrated this each Sunday: people putting chairs out, praying with others, preaching, cooking food, expressing hospitality, sharing the Lord's Supper together and baptizing new believers. Because of this, I naturally thought of Christ's body in terms of its work. But on that first Sunday after Edith's death, I saw something a lot richer than before.

Christ's body, like all of ours, doesn't only exist to work. No – bodies cry, share and love, just as Jesus cried, shared and loved when he had a physical body. It's by our physical presence that we extend compassion and comfort, through our words and our hugs, or just by sitting there in the sadness. And since the time when Jesus ascended to heaven, leaving his earthly body, he left his Holy Spirit to 'form one body' and to minister his very real presence through the love, gifts and service of his new body, the church.

Joanna and I wanted to experience Jesus' love and comfort, but seeing his people felt hard. On that first Sunday, however, God's presence with us was so apparent, ministered to us through our church family. While the other Jonny preached on Jesus crying with mourners around Lazarus's grave, we could see Jesus' tears being cried in the eyes of his people. As we were reminded of God's comfort to those mourning, the arms of Jesus hugged, held and upheld us through the many who rushed our way. We didn't only hear about the hope of the renewed world; we saw a glimpse of it, in the renewed hearts of our brothers and sisters, desperate to bring some healing that will one day be complete in the new creation.

All Christians want Christ in their suffering but few want the church. But to distance ourselves from Jesus' body would be to distance ourselves from Jesus himself – our Lord who weeps for us, comforts us, heals us and loves us eternally.

When I was a kid, I broke my arm. Although it wasn't particularly useful to me while it healed, my broken arm didn't stop being part of my body. In the same way, when the trauma of baby loss comes our way, or any kind of suffering, we don't stop being parts of Jesus' body because we are broken. But, unlike my arm, when we are broken our service to church and beyond becomes *more* effective. Of course, Joanna and I were naturally taken off all church rotas indefinitely, but Jesus still has a very special ministry role for sufferers within his body.

When we lost Edith, both Christians and non-Christians were watching: the midwives we prayed in front of, members of the church, friends, family and work colleagues at the funeral . . . Whether we liked it or not, we were on show, and people were silently asking how we'd respond to this crisis. *Will they walk away from God? Isn't this evidence that God is either not there or he's not good? Will they keep talking about God's goodness now?*

When we neither walked away nor denied God's constant goodness, the Holy Spirit was communicating something through us that he has always communicated through his suffering people: that in our weakness, Jesus alone is our strength. Despite our many tears, people would often say that we were so strong. We would respond by saying, 'You're not seeing our strength – we're completely broken and weak. You're seeing Jesus' strength in us.'

While I wasn't preaching or leading Bible studies, the simple act of worship – sitting among brothers and sisters, plodding on and affirming our gospel hope – was speaking far more clearly than any sermon I'd delivered. Suffering's sermon is this: despite losing everything, Jesus is enough. Standing in church, singing 'All I have is Christ', people knew we meant it. Not giving up on God in our suffering served them by confirming what we all know to be true but so often doubt: he is worthy of our praise, no matter what happens in our lives. The Lord gives, and he takes away. Blessed be the name of the Lord.

It was no coincidence that, only weeks after Edith's death, I read this passage in my Bible: 'I rejoice in what I am suffering *for you*, and I fill up in my flesh what is still lacking in regard to Christ's afflictions, *for the sake of his body*, which is the church' (Colossians 1:24, my emphasis).

In our suffering, we needed the church to minister Christ's presence and comfort to us. But despite our pain we were still parts of God's body, and the church still needed us to minister to *them*. And this, not from a position of strength, but from a position of brokenness.

Joanna

Going to church that first Sunday was a real gift, but we couldn't do services of lament for the whole year ahead. Inevitably the shock of what had happened wore off as the weeks and months went by. Before long, things went back to normal, for others but not for us, for we were only just beginning to grieve.

At times, church felt really difficult. As much as I loved our church family, this was a place full of redeemed and recovering sinners, like Jonny and me. Through ignorance, insensitivity or simply inexperience of situations like ours, my brothers and sisters had the potential to hurt me. With so many mums in such a small space, I was scared that I'd either overhear or find myself in a conversation about sleepless nights or feeding troubles, when I would have given anything for those to have been my problems. One mum mentioned that her worst nightmare would be to give birth in public. But I'd have given up all my dignity if it meant that I could hear even one of Edith's cries. For me, my worst nightmare was giving birth to my dead daughter, the nightmare that had become my life.

I knew that I had impossible expectations of people at church. If they were slow to ask how I was doing, I thought that they didn't care or that Edith had already been forgotten. But if they asked me out of the blue how grief was going, I felt put on the spot, unable to readily articulate the complexity of my pain and hope in Jesus. I often settled for a cursory, 'It's OK, thank you – hard, but I'm doing OK.' For sure it was hard, but I wasn't doing OK.

Because I thought that no one else in church had experienced baby loss, I felt alone. My sense of belonging to the body of Christ felt weakened in comparison to my sense of belonging to an imagined community of grieving mums who would surely 'get me'. I was unaware that there were members of our church who had in fact lost children, but I was also initially unaware of how I was looking to people to offer the comfort that only Jesus can give. Yes, the church was his body – but asking them to be my Saviour, Healer and Sustainer was to place an unliftable weight on their shoulders. Doing this, and seeing them inevitably fail, would only grow a root of bitterness in my heart. Looking to Jesus, however, I was freed from looking to my friends to be for me what only he can be. There I found a liberty to invite them into my grief – something I had found myself naturally avoiding.

Safe in Jesus' understanding, presence and love, I was able no longer to answer people's question with: 'It's hard, but I'm doing OK, thanks.' I could freely say that I wasn't coping, that the days felt impossible and that the thought of my daughter's body decaying in the ground five miles away was torturing me throughout the night. With Jesus' understanding and love secure, whether their response mirrored his love or displayed a British awkwardness mattered far less. They weren't the Saviour: Jesus was. And this new-found freedom and willingness to be honest about the pain seemed to burst a bubble of social convention that was standing in the way of spiritual communion. I began to be proactive in seeking out opportunities to cry in community.

I asked my friend Kath if she'd like to spend some time together, looking at Edith's box of keepsakes that we'd gathered from our time with her in hospital. Of course, I expected her to say 'yes' as a way to comfort me in my grief, but I didn't expect her to give me a hug, cry on my shoulder and say that she'd hadn't known whether to ask me first. That week, we sat on the sofa and looked at Edith's clay foot imprint. We flicked through photographs, taken in Abby Suite 2. Taking a lock of her auburn hair out of a plastic pocket, Kath wept as she held it next to mine for its unmistakeable similarity. She stroked Edith's fox sleep suit, which still had on it the pale marks of her weeping skin. She straightened out the tape-measure that Mikaela had used to mark her length and head circumference. Far from looking to Kath to be my saviour, crying together on a sofa was a picture of how God's people are navigating this grief-stricken world together. None of us can be for each other what only Jesus is, and yet Jesus uses us to be his hands and feet, his mind and his heart towards the broken-hearted. Just like on the evening of Edith's birth and that first Sunday at church, allowing others into our pain opened us up to Jesus' healing in our lives.

As I grew more confident to invite others in, they also became more forthcoming towards me and our situation. Another friend, Anneli, showed up with a roll of sugar paper and some board pens. She wanted to come and pray with me, to get all of the emotions out on the paper, before bringing it all to God. It was an act of kindness towards me, but it was also for her. Although Edith was my daughter, because the church is a family it really was true that others were grieving. As Paul writes, using the body analogy that we saw earlier: 'If one part suffers, every part suffers with it' (1 Corinthians 12:26).

These episodes of shared grief, and many others, would never have happened so long as I responded to questions about my grief with: 'It's hard, but I'm doing OK, thank you.' This closes down conversation in fear of an imperfect response. Putting on a brave face would only say to others, 'I'm OK – I'm strong.' But crying uncontrollably through every song on Sunday spoke loudly and clearly: 'I'm not OK. But because I know Jesus is mine, and he's here with me in the pain, I can show and share my suffering with you.'

If Satan had one plan for my grief, it was to convince me that pain relief consisted in moving away from God's people. But in his grace God overruled and ministered his love to me in a very real way – through the hands and hearts of his church, the body of his suffering Son.

'Resignation' (Part 1)

by Henry Wadsworth Longfellow

There is no flock, however watched and tended,
But one dead lamb is there!
There is no fireside, howsoe'er defended,
But has one vacant chair!

The air is full of farewells to the dying,
And mournings for the dead;
The heart of Rachel, for her children crying,
Will not be comforted!

Let us be patient! These severe afflictions
Not from the ground arise,
But oftentimes celestial benedictions
Assume this dark disguise.

We see but dimly through the mists and vapors;
Amid these earthly damps
What seem to us but sad, funereal tapers
May be heaven's distant lamps.

There is no Death! What seems so is transition;
This life of mortal breath
Is but a suburb of the life elysian,
Whose portal we call Death.

She is not dead, – the child of our affection, –
But gone unto that school
Where she no longer needs our poor protection,
And Christ himself doth rule.[5]

7

Being a man, grieving a child

Jonny

The room was different but, two months on, the cream walls brought it all back. Joanna and I held hands on a plastic sofa beneath a wall clock stuck at quarter-past two. One of the bereavement midwives brought through a tray of coffee and digestive biscuits before sitting opposite.

Alison asked questions and Joanna answered. I smiled, putting in the odd word here and there, but before long I realized I'd zoned out. Alison had just asked a question that I didn't hear.

'It's OK if you can't put it into words,' she said, as I regained concentration. 'This is still so fresh, and it will be a process of many years before things might become clearer.' Alison was nodding encouragingly as I looked to Joanna for her response. But Joanna had already turned towards me, as though also waiting for mine.

'Oh, sorry – were you talking to *me*?' I asked Alison.

'Yes. How do *you* feel?'

I was back in the room . . . How did I feel? I wasn't sure. Over the last few months, Joanna and I had entered this new world of sympathetic midwives, counselling schedules and a house that resembled a fully stocked florist's. But this was more Joanna's world than mine. Of course, there was always a seat for me in the corner while midwives swarmed around

Joanna's hospital bed, always a tissue for me if I needed it, albeit housed in a floral box next to potpourri, and the constant reminder that 'sometimes men need counselling too'. But in this new world of support for grieving mums, I didn't know how to be a grieving dad. And yet here I was, being asked how I felt.

'I feel like I'm in a new world,' I ventured, buying myself some time to think through a fuller response. 'To be honest, I don't really know what I'm doing or what I *should* be doing – what's healthy and what's not. I'm just . . . well . . . keeping on going. Does that make sense?'

Alison stifled a sad smile. 'It absolutely makes sense. Most dads I speak to say they don't know how to deal with the emotion of it all. But what you're doing now, simply by talking about your emotions, is really healthy.'

I wasn't impressed with myself. I had never really fitted the 'guy stereotype' of not being comfortable with emotions. I assumed I'd be fine. I assumed I *was* fine. My focus was simply to make sure that Joanna was well looked after and given the right space to grieve in a healthy and spiritually productive way. But the coming months revealed that I wasn't as self-aware as I thought I was; in fact, I fitted the 'guy stereotype' down to a tee.

Ten years before Edith died, I was completely sold on the Bible's vision for Christian husbands: 'Husbands, love your wives, just as Christ loved the church and gave himself up for her' (Ephesians 5:25).

The daily commitment of a husband to carry his bride's burden and give himself up for her was a beautiful picture of God's love for us in Jesus in the letter to the Ephesians. In fact,

I loved it so much that one reason I pursued marriage was so that I could play my part in this great gospel witness to a watching world. While the daily reality of dying to myself wasn't so idyllic after marrying Joanna – where did I ever get the idea that death would be pretty? – I never lost my desire to be a little picture, albeit a very imperfect one, of Jesus laying down his life for his bride. I always wanted to carry Joanna's burden, and the day Edith died the heaviest burden she'd ever been called to carry had been placed squarely on her shoulders. Therefore, for me, the job at hand was obvious. Being godly in this situation meant lifting as much of that burden as I possibly could. So I got to work.

Before long, my life had become a flurry of burden-lifting activity. I took Josiah to the park daily so Joanna could write down her emotions. I planned expensive date-nights as opportunities to spoil her. I prayed long into the night for God to mend her broken heart. My intentions were good: I wanted to obey God's call on my life through this ordeal to love Joanna like Jesus and to carry her burden as Christ had carried mine. But no matter how much we pursue obedience in self-sacrifice, sometimes we can pursue it disobediently or in a way that still serves ourselves. At the time, I wasn't aware that this flurry of activity served my own ends, despite being dressed up as carrying Joanna's burden. I wanted to distract myself, and her, from our pain, and doing stuff was the best way to do it.

I left the house with Josiah because I couldn't deal with seeing Joanna in so much pain. I spent money on date-nights so we could talk about the nice surroundings while drinking fancy drinks, instead of sipping tea in our front room where the gaping hole at the heart of our home felt so palpable. I prayed for Joanna away from her, so the outpouring of emotion to God would not jar with the calm, domestic environment I was so keen to maintain.

My attempt to carry her pain was only adding to it. She felt isolated when she sat alone with her pen and pad. She also felt alone when I was flitting around, cooking meals but never sitting down and seeing her sad eyes. 'Carrying her burden' had become to me synonymous with the pursuit of putting a smile on Joanna's face, when what she really needed was for me to sit with her in the sadness, to hug her while she sobbed. I was acting as though grief could be by-passed, as though, if I did enough for her and bought her enough treats, one day we'd wake up and our home would no longer feel the absence of our little girl, the future we'd lost would now be a happy present and we would have refound our happy-ever-before. We'd pick up then where we'd left off.

I had bought into my culture's view that being strong looks like standing tall. But if Jesus is our model of strength, being strong means staring grief in the face of those we love, and being weak and broken in its shadow. So long as I couldn't confront my own grief, I could never comfort Joanna in hers. So long as I wanted to appear strong, I'd only ever be a weak man, unable to shoulder some of the burden for my struggling wife and unable to love her as Jesus did, and does.

But in his patient grace, six months on, God brought this façade of strength crashing down to the ground. As is his habit, he had plans for renovation.

It was a wet and windy Wednesday. Before leaving the office to catch my train, I put my earphones in and fired up Spotify. The sliding office doors opened automatically, revealing a wild April storm. I braced myself, putting up my hood, before the music in my ears suddenly stopped, replaced by a man's voice. *That's odd*, I thought. *Spotify waits for the end of songs to play ads.* Taking my phone out of my pocket, I saw that Spotify had been replaced by an amateur video with the BBC News icon in the bottom corner. A man with a north-west accent was speaking about Charlie's Child Loss Charity. 'Charlie was eight pounds two. I held him and I cut his cord. Like most men, I thought I had to be the strong one, but soon I realized I was spiralling into a deep depression.'

It was nothing I hadn't heard before. But it was like God had stopped me in my tracks and beamed in an average-looking guy in his late twenties from Oldham to raise me from my slumber and to make me feel the emotions I'd spent six months denying. Alison's words came back to me: 'Most dads say they don't know how to deal with the emotion of it all.' Why did I think I wouldn't be one of 'most dads'? Perhaps it was an arrogant confidence in my emotional intelligence, or a self-reliance to shoulder this for Joanna. Whatever God was pinpointing, the mask fell off and I saw what I'd been hiding all along.

Battered by gusts of wind, I wept and wept. My tears were masked by the rain, my cries drowned out by the wind and passing cars ploughing through puddles. Despite the sheer weight of emotion, it was a weight that was now falling off me. With every tear, a sense of relief filled up the space where it had been stored.

I arrived at the station and stood waiting for my train, but the tears didn't stop there. I got into the quiet carriage, forcing myself to calm down, but the tears flowed even more. Twenty minutes later I got off at my station and walked through Birmingham city centre. But six months of grief weren't finished yet. They had found a fault-line in my defences and simply would not stop until every tear that I hadn't cried finally found its way out.

It wasn't until about an hour and a half later that I'd run out of crying. But now I was finally ready to grieve – finally ready to go back to my grief-stricken home, my grief-stricken wife, and face the situation for what it was.

Unlike other grief, the death of a child brings an equal measure of pain to both parents. There's no clear line between mourner and comforter. Both mum and dad are mourners *and* comforters. Realizing that I too had to mourn the loss of Edith was the first stage of the grief process for me, and yet this was also the necessary step that enabled Joanna also to move forward in her grief.

Yes, we all grieve differently. But my failure to mourn such deep suffering meant that Joanna could only go so far. So long as the culture of our home remained plastic and my speediness to move on to brighter topics of conversation persisted, Joanna could only ever feel alone in her sadness. Suffering, which should have united us in our shared pain, had actually driven a wedge between Joanna and her hiding husband. But I was now keen to change all that.

Arriving home on that wet Wednesday, I took Joanna by the hand, sat down on the sofa and sobbed on her shoulder. Crying uncontrollably demolished the façade of strength I'd managed to keep up since returning from the hospital six months before. And yet perhaps falling into Joanna's arms in a broken heap of weakness was my greatest display of strength since Edith had died. In any case, the strength to do so wasn't my own. It came from elsewhere.

But [God] said to me, 'My grace is sufficient for you, for my power is made perfect in weakness.' Therefore I will boast all the more gladly about my weaknesses, so that Christ's power may rest on me. That is why, for Christ's sake, I delight in weaknesses, in insults, in hardships, in persecutions, in difficulties. For when I am weak, then I am strong.

(2 Corinthians 12:8–10)

If the apostle Paul, that intrepid missionary, leader and mentor, so significant in the New Testament church, needed his strength to be broken down into weakness before he could serve God's people rightly, how much more did I need to sit in the rubble of my own strength and self-reliance before I could serve my wife? Yes, I wanted to love Joanna like Jesus loved her. But for me to grasp Christ's power, I had to remember that he displayed his power by the weakness of being nailed to a cross. Where did I get the idea that I could love Joanna like Jesus without being made weak? Without admitting my own lack of strength to be for her what she needed?

And that was the problem. I was so confident that I could be for her what she needed. My desire to be like Jesus was actually a confidence in my own ability, to *be* Jesus for her. Jesus was who Joanna needed – not me. 'He must become greater; I must become less,' said John the Baptist, who 'prepared the way of the Lord', one of the strongest men to ever have lived. That must be the refrain of Christian husbands in the throes of shared grief: *to love my wife, I must be seen for the broken man that I am, and Jesus must be seen for the rock of strength that he is.*

As I sobbed on Joanna's shoulder, she too began to cry. There was a warmth in her embrace and an intimacy that my façade of strength had inhibited. Two grieving parents, crying together, had torn down the tension of playing domestic make-believe. This wasn't OK. I wasn't OK, and neither was Joanna. And because my weakness had been laid bare, like Paul I was able to find a new strength – not one from the recesses of my own spiritual power but, in the absence of any such power, this was a strength I gladly drew from Another. As the psalmist says, 'Blessed is the one who takes refuge [in the Lord]' (Psalm 34:8).

As we pulled away from one another and wiped our eyes with pulled-down sleeves, I looked squarely into Joanna's mascara-stained face. Still slightly choking on my breath, I simply asked her how she felt – a question I'd asked hundreds of times. But this was no longer an emotional tick-box exercise to convince myself I had done my duty. She knew by the tone of my voice that this time I actually wanted to hear the answer; I wanted to hear about the pain and share in it. Of course, hearing about her wounds would wound me further. But when you're no longer relying on your own strength, these wounds can do no damage. Confident that God's strength was strong enough to bear the load of our combined grief, I was empowered to hear the deepest depths of my precious wife's pain and no longer be overwhelmed.

'For when I am weak, then I am strong.'

God's strength wasn't only power to hear the heartbreak of my wife, but also to do the very thing I'd set out to do but failed in. Once I was no longer flitting around in a frenzy of activity to carry Joanna's burden, the security I'd found in

God's strength enabled me to serve her as I had intended. I still made dinners; I still took Josiah to the park to give her space; I still treated her. But these things were no longer a way to avoid the pain. Content in my own weakness, and confident in the Lord's strength, Joanna now felt free to say whether she wanted to talk, or to be alone, or to have some space, or to make the dinner herself. Relying on God's strength created a new household culture where our pain was evident for all to see, and yet Joanna and I were united in it, united to Christ, who was upholding us every step of the way.

I was changed for good after that stormy episode at the train station. I still had, and still have, the tendency to bottle things up, sometimes without realizing it. But, no longer having to be the strong one, I became proactive with my own grief. I needed to coax the cooped-up emotion out of me. Sometimes that simply meant praying for myself, as well as Joanna. Even when I didn't feel an urge, I would sit down with Edith's memory box or listen to Arvo Pärt. Only with such deliberate action would I be able to *feel* the emotion that was hiding away below the surface.

I'd previously seen this time investment as self-serving and not carrying Joanna's cross for her like Jesus did. But only by confronting and confessing my own grief could I bring any kind of comfort to Joanna. Six months into running a pretty tight ship, this felt like a kind of death. But after all, isn't death the Bible's vision for Christian husbands? Christ laid down his life for his bride, the church, so whether in good times or bad – in sickness or in health – there is no other way.

Bad times were now our new normal, but laying down my life emotionally for Joanna would be necessary for what would happen next.

Interlude: the only son of his mother

Shuffling sandals vied for space under the murmuring hub-bub. Children jumped up amid the swirling sea of heads to catch a glimpse of the crowd's captain. But Jesus didn't look back. He wasn't heading to Nain to do party tricks. He had work to do.

As Jesus approached the town gate, a commotion spilled out. A wooden stretcher appeared, carried on men's shoulders, with a lifeless body on top. Around them family members of the dead waved scarves in the air and wept into their sleeves. Jesus stopped to allow the funeral procession to pass by, at which point he noticed that the man on the stretcher was hardly more than a boy, still dressed in yesterday's clothes – a dirty shawl and some sandals with a broken strap. His face shone white in the afternoon sun.

'Catch her, catch her!' cried one of the pallbearers. A woman immediately behind them – the boy's mother – let out a loud gasp and fell back into the arms of two onlookers. She hadn't fainted with the heat, but with grief. First her husband, and now her only son. What did she have left? No income, no stability, but above all no hope. She was alone in the world.

Jesus watched as the woman opened her glazed eyes before being lifted back on to her feet. Bending over to grasp her knees and regain composure, the pain of being woken up returned to her stricken face. Jesus' heart filled with compassion, as though her pain were his own.

Without introduction or words of condolence, he looked at her and said, 'Don't cry' – not a command against her tears, but the overflow of a father's heart for his daughter. *'Don't cry.'*

Still bent over, the woman slowly lifted her head towards Jesus. His words to her were not only the fruits of compassion but somehow a promise. Hope seemed to hang in the air. *Who is this man? What does he have to do with me?* The widow considered moving on, but her feet were pinned to the dust and her eyes fixed on to his, as if something new was dawning in her life – a new reality beyond the shadow of family grief. It was near, and yet she couldn't quite grasp it. Jesus walked towards her and she finally stood upright. While still looking into her eyes, Jesus touched the stretcher and spoke calmly, as though to the widow.

'Young man, I say to you, get up.'

The boy sat up, and the woman's face crumpled in front of him. Jesus took the boy by the fingers and handed him back to his mother. She hugged her son and kissed his dirty hair. The crowd reacted with fear and amazement.

'God has come to help his people!' they shouted, swarming around Jesus. But he moved on swiftly through the town gate, before the widow even had time to ask his name.

'He's Joseph's son, from Nazareth,' she heard someone say. His words continued to circle in her mind.

Don't cry. Don't cry. He said, 'Don't cry.' It was as if Jesus had promised her the world – and in a way, he had. He had given back the world she'd lost. And yet the lingering feeling after meeting this man from Nazareth was that he'd given her a new world, a future for which she would now wait.

PART 1: WEEPING

PART 2: WALKING

PART 3: WAITING

Excerpt from Joanna's diary

17 December 2018

Yesterday and today have been hard. I just wanted to be at thirty-seven weeks with another baby. I want to be in labour, ready to meet my child. I want to be cuddling, holding, feeding. I don't want to have to wait. I don't want the fear and anxiety of living the thirty-seven weeks. I don't want the uncertainty of when we might or might not get pregnant, and I don't want to face the possibility of miscarriage. I want a full home, kids running around and enjoying their siblings. I want Edith alive and at home with us.

8

Hoping for rainbows

Joanna

'How late are you?' asked Jonny, with an expectant smile. Josiah was sipping a babyccino and rolling around on the sofa. In the open thoroughfare of a shopping centre, this coffee shop had become a weekly fixture where Josiah could run free and where we could process the emotions of the day.

'I don't know . . .' I said, genuinely clueless about the movements of my menstrual cycle so soon after giving birth. 'Last month was the first cycle since Edith and it came on day twenty-six, but it's probably just readjusting itself.'

'That's short, though,' Jonny replied, leaning back in his high-backed chair. 'And today is . . . ?'

'Day twenty-seven,' I interrupted. My quick response probably gave away my nervousness and excitement about the possibility of being pregnant again. What I didn't tell Jonny was that I really *felt* pregnant – either that or I was getting an unusual amount of period pain. *Am I being silly?* I thought. What if this was all in my head? We'd conceived Edith after one month, but that was unlikely to happen twice. Wasn't it?

'We'll just have to wait and see,' said Jonny, peering over my head to check on Jos as I scooped up the milk froth from the bottom of my cup. 'We just shouldn't get our hopes up.'

But our hopes were already up – having hope is the default position of all our hearts. Since I was a little girl, I'd always hoped for a full home, with many mouths to feed and many hearts to fill. When Edith died, this hope seemed to be buried with her. *Would Josiah be an only child? How many more miscarriages or stillbirths would follow? Did God have a different plan for my life?* If he did, I didn't want it.

Staring at the evening shoppers and commuters walking purposefully past, I wondered how many had experienced baby loss – and how many had gone on to have 'rainbow babies'. A rainbow child would never replace Edith, but perhaps God would soon restore to me the hope of a bustling family life. It was the waiting – the not knowing – that was hardest. I put my spoon in the cup and looked up to see Jonny staring sincerely back at me, almost probing a response.

'Yeah, let's just wait and see,' I replied, feigning calmness and patience. In reality, I just longed to be back on that delivery ward at Birmingham Women's Hospital, about to meet my baby. In short, I was hoping for a rainbow.

Waking up the next morning, there was still no sign of my period. By lunch, still nothing. Jonny didn't want to ask me every hour if it had come, so each time I entered a room he'd look round to see if I was OK. When it was obvious I hadn't received bad news, he'd relax. But it was tense; we were tense. We'd speak about our day, but we really wanted to speak about how many days late I was. We asked who should pick up Jos from nursery, but we really wanted to ask who should pick up a pregnancy test from the supermarket. We couldn't . . . not yet. To jump the gun and get a negative test would only increase the sense of loss. We learned to live with an elephant in the room, following us wherever we went, sitting with us at the dinner table and lying between us as we prayed before bed.

But when another day ticked over, I just had to call the elephant out. We were out with close friends who were encouraging us to wait patiently through grief for heaven, while all I could think about was how impatiently I was waiting through grief for another baby. I had to bring it up again with Jonny when we got back – surely it was late enough now to broach the question? So when we arrived home, I went upstairs and closed the bathroom door behind me. If it hadn't come now, we just had to do a test . . .

But it had come. And I cried and cried.

Jonny

The bereavement midwives had told us that we'd probably fall into one of two groups of grieving parents: those who wanted to try for another baby right away and those who simply couldn't face the possibility of carrying another loss. Some doctors advised us to wait until the results of the post-mortem. Others dismissed that, advising that we should try when the time was right for us. In the thick fog of contradictory medical advice, all we could do was head for the light. For Joanna and me, the only light we could make out in grief's shadow was that of holding another baby in our arms. Short of bringing Edith back, there was nothing we wanted more.

Before that time, I'd always thought grief and hope were on opposite sides of the emotion spectrum. It took Edith's death for me to realize how wrong I was. Grief and hope are like new lovers, having recently met by some chance and now impossible to separate. Whenever grief turned up, hope was there with it – hope of better times ahead, and of regaining what had been lost.

In our grief, we'd never hoped so much for another baby. We longed to hear those newborn cries and feel the clasp of tiny fingers around ours. In some ways, this hope kept us going and gave us the motivation to get out of bed in the morning. Friends spoke about this as a positive sign of being on the road to recovery. However, despite giving us the motivation to put one foot in front of the other, longing for another baby did nothing to heal us. The more we hoped for another baby, the more we looked for some assurance that it would happen. And because no one could promise this, when our hope weighed heavy we were only pushed deeper into the throes of grief – an inescapable cycle towards hopelessness.

Everything felt so fragile. What if God said 'No' to another? What if we did get pregnant . . . how would we make it through nine months of going to bed not knowing if Joanna would miscarry or have another stillbirth? What if God gave us another baby but then something happened to Jos? *The Lord gives, and he takes away.* Finding solid ground, when the rug of our lives had just been pulled from under our feet, felt near impossible.

Of course, hope can be a healthy sign in grief's gloom, but it has to be the right kind of hope – one that doesn't stand on sinking sand, but on solid rock. Our lives amount to little more than holding on to some kind of hope, but the Bible has a very strange category of the sinking-sand kind of hope that grievers are prone to, and that I was beginning to put my trust in. It's the kind of hope that we can hold on to tightly, but that will ultimately leave us without hope.

God's Word says that, without Jesus, we humans are '*without hope* and without God in the world' (Ephesians 2:12, my emphasis). After suffering the loss of one of God's good gifts, who wouldn't be prone to finding hope in regaining that gift? Whether we look to what we've lost or something else, grieving will always mean finding hope in something. And because it's all that we know, we tend to look for this hope 'in the world'. But with its many gifts of God's grace, this world is the very place where God says that lasting hope can't be found. If our deepest hope is here, we're ultimately without God, and without hope in a world that can't give it to us. With Jesus, however, we find what we're looking for: our hope is transferred from this world to the future world that Jesus promises his followers. Unlike our hopes, pinned to our present home, this is a world that 'does not disappoint' (Romans 5:5, NKJV).

It's no coincidence that when the apostle Peter writes his famous description of the hope Jesus offers, he writes it to grieving Christians like you and me, prone to shift our hope on to sand. We grieve for our children, and so hope for another baby. But, to our despair, that hope can die overnight. It has once, or perhaps twice, and it might do again. So Peter points towards our future hope in Jesus as a 'living hope . . . that can never perish, spoil or fade' (1 Peter 1:3–4) – this hope *can't* die. He writes:

> In all this you greatly rejoice, though now for a little while you may have had to suffer grief in all kinds of trials. These have come so that the proven genuineness of your faith – of greater worth than gold, which

113

perishes even though refined by fire – may result in praise, glory and honour when Jesus Christ is revealed. (1 Peter 1:6–7)

Unlike many well-meaning friends who encouraged us with the likelihood that we'd have more children, Peter points to a hope that isn't based on statistics; it isn't here in this world, but it's 'kept in heaven' for us (1 Peter 1:4). Our perseverance through grief grows in us our heavenly hope, so that when we die Jesus will be praised, and we will finally take hold of what we always hoped to find in this world.

There's no short cut to this solid-rock kind of hope. For me, it was only when I found myself desperately holding on to the hope of another baby, and finding it to be hopelessly insufficient, that God began to work. Over the following months, he continued that work, not to take my hope away but to slowly replace it with a better one.

Joanna

When I was able to keep back the tears, I sat in the bathroom, head in hands. I felt stupid for ever thinking I could be pregnant. Dragging my heels downstairs into the living room, I saw Jonny turn to look at me, but this time seeing what he had feared. As he stood up, no words were necessary. I leaned my head into his shoulder, he wrapped his arms around my waist, and we stood there, crying silently for some time – a tragic scene that seemed to repeat itself over and over again as the months slipped by, chasing away whatever hope we had left.

Every month I wasn't pregnant was a fresh flashback to finding out I was no longer pregnant with Edith. The waiting . . . the fear . . . the test. 'Negative' was the verdict on my womb, but also on my life. It was our monthly reminder of losing our little girl who had once been tucked up inside me. 'Negative.' Like a rumbling stomach, desperate to be filled, the emptiness of my womb seemed to cry out for Edith but was forced to starve. Edith was gone, and new life felt like water in a parched land.

Jesus has promised to establish his new world where there will be no loss, no tears, no death. This is Christian hope, and this had been my hope since I was a little girl, putting my trust in Jesus for the first time. But it didn't stop other hopes – sometimes rival hopes – taking root in my heart. My desire to be a mum to many was a good hope, but had it grown into something that I needed in order to live the good and fulfilled life? Perhaps. Perhaps it was one of many hopes I had for my life that I simply expected God would give me and which, in my mind, would challenge his goodness if he withheld it. Hope for my life had ultimately shifted to this world, and as a Christian I always believed God would straighten out those desires. In fact, this was why I thought God had taken Edith away.

In some ways, we all relate to God as a cosmic cashier, dispensing good gifts for the godly and withholding them from the rebels. This is why people like me, so aware of our sin and worldly hopes, expect to be treated harshly by God – a heavenly Father who always has the rod of discipline in his hands to correct his wayward children. Being painfully aware that I wanted Edith back more than I wanted the God who was always mine, the questions and accusations began to rage.

Perhaps this is why God took Edith, I thought. *God had to wake me up to show me where I'm putting my trust, and he lovingly wants to realign my heart towards him and the hope of heaven.* And if God would withhold another baby from me until I'd got my priorities sorted out, I wasn't going to get pregnant any time soon. God knew my heart: he knew how much I wanted a baby and how little comfort the new creation brought me in my grief. Trying to conjure up a greater love for him was futile – after all, wasn't I doing it simply to get something from God? Rather than relating to the God of grace who works in all things for our good, I'd turned him into a cosmic cashier, ready to do a transaction with me once I had the spiritual cash to pay for what I wanted from him. But in God's economy, babies are not bargaining chips. And neither is our spiritual growth.

I now realized that misunderstanding what God is like always leads to us being robbed of hope and joy. When confronted by my wayward affections, my misplaced hopes and my faulty reasoning, I didn't naturally run into God's gracious arms, stretched wide because Jesus had once stretched his arms wide for me on a cross. No, I simply felt broken. The grief was bad enough, but because of what it had dug up in my heart I felt the added burden of my sin pushing down on me – crushing me – before the all-knowing and holy God.

Of course, this didn't stop me from having hope. Feeling sinful, and less assured of my heavenly hope, I turned to lesser hopes to provide me with a quick fix to feeling broken. I wanted to go shopping and splash cash that I didn't have.

I wanted to gorge my way through endless slabs of chocolate. Perhaps we needed to do a round-the-world tour? Or do something crazier, like the people on TV who go and live completely off-grid . . . ? Perhaps there – in the shopping bags, the comfort, the experiences and the new life – I would find my elusive hope.

But because God had planted his Word deep in me from childhood, I knew this was folly. The shopping didn't fix my heart. The chocolate was great, but without God I was left feeling empty. The world was hollowed of hope, so I only had the option of looking beyond this world to find the hope that was never to be found here. God continually brought me back to where true hope is found, and it was at this point that God's gracious promise, not only to create a new and perfect world but also to give it to sinners with all of our disordered desires, had never felt more real.

Rather than conjuring up a love for God and a hope of heaven in my own strength, God was the One at work to realign my heart and my hope. He didn't take Edith because I had it all wrong. He wasn't doing a transaction. It's hardly surprising that the idea of an eternity with a harsh Father, or a cosmic cashier, made me, and countless others, waver in our gospel hope. God is a kind Father who gives true hope to people who are doing everything to find heaven without him. Only with the right view of God, not only in my head but also in my heart, could I begin to grow in my love for him, and in my hope of spending eternity with him.

While God was at work untangling and reordering my hopes, the simpler day-to-day grief grew particularly deep and dark. At night, I would have nightmares about Edith's decaying body in the ground. I would wake up shaking, the images continuing to swirl around my head. While this felt separate from God's work in my life, these visual reminders of what was happening to my little girl were not outside God's plan to replace my worldly hopes with a better one. After all, weren't these images of decay as clear a picture as any of where my worldly hopes will end up, buried under six feet of dirt? Why invest my hope in what's destined for decay?

When our hope in another baby sat heaviest on our shoulders, we were pushed downwards into the mire of grief, into what we'd lost in this world. But as painful as the images of decay were, God was causing me to look upwards towards our only hope that could answer the grief – not towards what we'd lost in Edith, but to what we'd gained in Jesus. Yes, Edith was buried in the ground and her body was decaying, but in her heavenly home she was enjoying the best this world has to offer, and far more. This is where God was calling me to invest my hope, and my empty womb was aching for it. My body was crying out in the same way as God's cursed world was crying out: 'in hope that the creation itself will be liberated from its bondage to decay' (Romans 8:20–21).

Liberation from decay comes only on the other side of death. Edith's body *had* to be planted in the ground so she could be raised up to be with God. With him, she has a new body that will never perish, spoil or fade. Paul writes:

> The body that is sown is perishable, it is raised imperishable; it is sown in dishonour, it is raised in glory; it is sown in weakness, it is raised in power; it is sown a natural body, it is raised a spiritual body.
> (1 Corinthians 15:42–44)

To take hold of life, we must endure death; that's where the Christian hope can be found. While this doesn't heal the wounds that grief inflicts, it does mean that we 'do not grieve like the rest of mankind, who have no hope' (1 Thessalonians 4:13). The hope of another pregnancy could only motivate us to keep going for a limited time. But knowing that Edith is safe with God and that we'll one day be with him – and her – empowers us to keep one foot in front of the other for the rest of our lives as we journey towards our true and lasting hope – the kingdom of God that lies beyond this world.

Jonny

'I want to test,' said Joanna, coming home to find me watching a glowing laptop screen. We'd been in this position a few times over the last six months. Joanna was possibly a few days late, but with moving goalposts each month as her cycle re-adjusted, we were limited to guesswork. 'I know we said we'd do it tomorrow, but I want to test now,' Joanna said resolutely, placing a shopping bag on the table and taking out a cellophane-wrapped pregnancy test.

Suddenly being faced with either a life-transforming event or another emotional kick to the stomach was quite a gear-change from watching *Match of the Day*. Six months of nil returns had taught me a lot about grief and hope, and here we were again – another God-given opportunity to grow in our trust of his plan.

I followed Joanna upstairs and we went through all the familiar motions before placing the test face down for sixty seconds. I held her waist as the seconds dragged like millstones around our necks. But when the time was up, we felt no freer to look.

'Let's just turn it over,' Joanna said. I let go of her waist, gave her a suppressed smile and turned it over.

Pregnant.

9

The happy ending?

Jonny

Last time I sat in this courtyard, the sky wasn't blue but a deep grey. I didn't notice then that the Abby Suite's Grief Garden was actually part of a larger space – one courtyard divided into two by a short fence and some shrubs. On the other side of the fence was the induction suite: a homely ward of smiling midwives and excited mums being induced into labour. Having come into this hospital for Edith, I'm not sure I would have appreciated looking over the fence to be taunted by the excitement of what felt like a world away – the world we'd just lost. I was then about five metres away from where I am now, on the other side of the fence, crying into my hands under a grave September sky. If I'd looked up and over the shrubs, the hope-filled hearts and the expectant smiles would, I'm sure, have caused me to get up and leave.

Perhaps you are reading this and you now feel that this is your time to leave. You sense the happy ending on the horizon, and you don't want to look over the fence either, to be taunted by the world you've lost. In your mind, these stories draw a dividing line, much higher than a short fence and some shrubs, between baby-loss sufferers and ex-baby-loss suf-ferers – those who've not gone on to have more children and those who have. Had I known fourteen months ago that today I'd be sitting on this side of the fence, looking through a large

121

glass window at Joanna propped up in a hospital bed, having received her first induction pessary, perhaps I'd have seen this as a happy ending too. But in reality, if this divided courtyard is any kind of metaphor, then right now I'm on the wrong side.

Over the fence, I can just about make out the words 'In Use' on Abby Suite 2's door, and I have the overwhelming sense that I belong over in the Grief Garden. Being hours away from hearing the cries of our little one hasn't relieved the grief; it's only intensified it, compounding the reminder of how real Edith was, how real our loss was and continues to be. Regardless of the blessing of so-called rainbow babies, after the trauma of loss, there is no full and final happy ending so long as we're in this world. *The grief never goes away.* If this garden is a metaphor of grief and hope, we need to get rid of the puny fence and shrubbery because, as we saw, grief and hope occupy the same space. What divides parents who've lost children isn't whether or not they go on to have more children, but whether they're still here in this world or are already with Jesus in his kingdom. For all of us parents still here, there's no graduation from grief, and no hope besides Jesus and the new world he promises. So long as we're this side of that new world, nothing will bring our little ones back. We're all just down here together, all in the same 'Grief Garden', and yet united in the hope that one day we'll see God, and the children we've lost.

I don't yet know the ending of our baby-loss story. What lies ahead in the coming hours, or maybe days, seems so precarious. But so long as this world is our home, there'll be no happy ending where all the mysterious and gut-wrenching threads are tied up and the purpose behind each one revealed. Not in our story either, and not in yours. So please don't leave.

The true happy ending of our story didn't change when Joanna actually fell pregnant, and hasn't changed over the following months either. If anything, the precariousness of this world has weighed even more heavily, and the happy ending that Jesus promises us has only come into sharper focus. So press on with us, we ask, as we journey home together.

Joanna

I picked up the pregnancy test for the third time in twenty minutes, checking the display once more.

'Joanna . . . it hasn't changed!' Jonny laughed. 'You're still pregnant.'

Both hearing the word 'pregnant' and seeing it on that little display seemed unbelievable. At the same time, the sense of emptiness over the previous months had felt so wrong, such that now 'pregnant' finally described not only how I felt but what I was. A burden was immediately lifted from my shoulders, and the fear that this moment would never come evaporated quickly, if only for those brief seconds. I looked at Jonny's relieved face, and I forced a smile in response. But the waves of disbelief, fear, joy and confusion that were rolling over me didn't distil naturally into a smile – or into any one display of emotion, for that matter. I didn't know what I was feeling, and Jonny could tell this too.

'Are you OK?' he asked, moving towards me with a confused look. It was clear that he felt a more straightforward excitement.

'I'm fine,' I replied, not telling the whole truth. I *was* fine, wasn't I? How could I not be fine, after hearing this amazing news? But 'fine' didn't cut it. Confusingly, I was weighed down by a new burden in the space left by the previous one, casting a shadow on what should indeed have been a joyful moment. Putting it into words felt almost impossible, as though saying it out loud increased the likelihood of it coming true. Jonny was still looking at me, patiently waiting for a response. I lifted my head to meet his eyes, and what had felt like a buried and unarticulated fear suddenly jumped off my tongue, as though desperate to make an escape:

'What if this baby dies too?'

The Lord gives, and he takes away. But would he do both in equal measure? He gave us Jos and he took Edith away. Would he give this child to us? In those first weeks, questions like these filled our minds. I knew I had to trust God, and yet second-guessing his plans came far more naturally. It felt like I'd stepped out of a dark world and into a dangerous one – a world that required more resilience and emotional energy than I had to give . . . perhaps even more than I had previously given, when my body had let go of Edith. The same feelings of guilt wasted no opportunity, and the self-blame reared its ugly head often. *What if I wasn't up to this? What if my body let another baby down? How could I ever cope with holding another lifeless child, peaceful yet painfully silent? How could I spend the rest of my life playing guessing games about the temperament and talents of another person? What about miscarriage?* Two stillbirths would be unlikely, but miscarriage didn't discriminate. One in four – perhaps five, at best – was lost before twenty-four weeks. What if we never even got to hold our child? How would I cope?

All of my emotional energy that grief hadn't spent on itself I had poured into getting pregnant. I hadn't even considered that, this side of a positive test, things might get *harder* during eight or nine long months of fear – months of waiting. Downloading an app that could predict my due date, I hoped to be pleasantly surprised, but 22 November seemed a lifetime away. Perhaps the doctors would induce me at thirty-seven weeks? But 1 November – my thirtieth birthday – didn't sound much better.

I just wanted to fall asleep, to close my eyes and wake up on my due date, bypassing the emotional trauma of the coming months. But any kind of escape from everyday life was impossible. Each morning, a two-year-old in the room across the hallway would wake up and need me to give him breakfast. The bathrooms still needed cleaning. Bills had to be paid. People would ask, 'How's the pregnancy going?' And I'd still respond, 'It's fine, thanks.' What else could I say? How could I spend the next eight months awkwardly articulating to colleagues and coffee baristas, insurance sellers and nursery workers, even friends and family, that I was on the edge of emotional collapse, unable to escape the unavoidable fact that this baby could die at any moment, just as Edith had? Where could I find any assurance that my baby was OK? I had extra scans, but Edith had died less than twenty-four hours after a sonographer described her scan as 'perfect'.

All the hopes I had placed in having another baby, and all the work God had done to begin fixing my eyes not on 1 November but on the new creation, were being channelled into, and exacerbated by, this new season. Sleep may have felt like the only refuge, but God's promises formed the place where he wanted to lead me . . . now more than ever.

Jonny

The Early Pregnancy Unit smelt the same, and the water dispenser still stood sadly in the corner of the waiting room, with *Woman's Weekly* sprawled across tables. We'd managed to get an early scan at seven weeks, simply to see our baby's heartbeat. The last time I'd seen one of those screens was when there was no heartbeat, when I could make out Edith's skull and her perfectly formed yet lifeless limbs. Compared to that, Joanna's womb looked like a vast expanse of space for this tiny ball of life, whose beating heart made my own heart skip a beat. The sonographer took some measurements and, with a smile on her face, announced that our child was in fact six weeks old, not seven. The news felt like a punch to the stomach, meaning that, after all the anxiety of the past week, we'd made no progress whatsoever. With an early induction date, we were coping with thirty weeks to go; thirty-one seemed one too many for us to deal with.

'It will come around soon enough,' said the sonographer – as did lots of our friends and family who, to our amazement, spoke confidently as if our baby 'will' be delivered safely. Their confidence served both as an encouraging corrective to our despondency and a discouraging reminder that, even after what had happened with Edith, people still underestimated the risk of baby loss. At worst we were told that, given what we'd been through, God wouldn't take another baby from us. Such ignorance mocked the pain of friends who'd suffered multiple miscarriages, and minimized how widely and how deeply the curse of sin has damaged every part of creation. God hadn't placed our suffering on a set of scales in order to determine what he'd do next; he hadn't promised us a rainbow baby because the last one was stillborn. What he had promised us was the hope of heaven, of being with him on the other side of this fallen world where pain and suffering rule the day. And before that day, God calls us, not to eager expectation of particular life circumstances, but to a life of patience through every suffering, while we wait for our certain hope. It was in the context of this kind of suffering that the apostle Paul wrote:

> For in this hope we were saved. But hope that is seen is no hope at all. Who hopes for what they already have? But if we hope for what we do not yet have, we wait for it patiently.
>
> (Romans 8:24–25)

We wait for it patiently. If God had promised that life wouldn't be hard, or that good times would neatly follow times of suffering, we wouldn't have to wait patiently. Who waits for what they already have? Why patience, if happiness is just around the corner? No – we wait patiently because the good times *are* coming, but they aren't here yet and won't be with us until we're with Jesus. Being called to patience assumes that we're desperately longing for that time but, instead, we so often set our minds on events and places in this world that, we hope, will be for us what only the new creation can ever be. And it was our desperate longing for our due date that God used as a powerful picture of what he calls us to in the Christian life – a patient, yet passionate, gaze towards the future, where our pain and suffering *will* come to an end.

If my impatience to get through this pregnancy felt this strong, how much more should I long for my new life in God's new world? Even with a safe delivery and a healthy child, anxiety and fear would live on here. No one could assure me that, once this baby was safely delivered, he or she'd be safe from cot death or severe pain or any number of debilitating medical conditions. And so, God's call to wait patiently for something so insecure made his call to wait patiently for my secure hope of heaven feel all the more pressing.

God didn't make us to live in a world of threat and fear. He didn't make us to be anxious, or to be scared of remaining childless, or to endure multiple baby losses. But that is the world we live in, and through the precariousness of our situation, and our eager expectation to meet our child, we grew in sync with God's cursed creation – this world which, itself, 'waits in eager expectation for the children of God to be revealed' (Romans 8:19). It's only when the world feels this scary and insecure that God graciously helps us to 'set our minds on things above' (Colossians 3:2) – where Christ is, and where there is safety and refuge, once and for all.

Joanna

I've often heard people say that God never gives us what we can't carry. But Jesus says something different. 'Whoever wants to be my disciple must deny themselves and take up their cross daily and follow me' (Luke 9:23).

When Jesus took up his cross, it was too heavy for him to carry. The Son of God, who holds the world in his hands, had to call on the help of another man to help shoulder his burden as he walked down the Calvary Road. And he says that if we want to follow him, we too will have to take up our cross –

something which will inevitably crush us under its weight, until we too learn to call for help.

The cross I was carrying *was* too heavy for me. The fear of losing another baby felt too difficult. Not only was this cross too heavy but the road was too long. If I couldn't manage to stand under the weight, how could I begin to walk with it on my shoulders, let alone make it down the long road to term? It sounds about right that God only gives us what we can carry, but God's very purpose is to give us what we *can't* carry, so that we learn how to depend on the strength that he alone gives for the journey home. Many carry the cross of child-lessness or of multiple miscarriages, sometimes for the rest of their lives. For me, even carrying the lighter cross of a rainbow pregnancy for a limited time meant having no other option than to cry out in desperate prayer to my heavenly Father.

We'd never prayed like we prayed for this baby, because never before had we felt our sheer powerlessness. When there's nothing you can do to keep your baby alive, you have to go to the only place – the only One – who holds that life, and yours, in his hands. God's tender reminder was that this was too big for us to carry on our own. And yet his call to take up our cross wasn't a cruel game, but his way of helping us to take steps forward in the power of his Holy Spirit and in the refuge of his fatherly care. Just as there was no way of having another child without walking this painful path ahead, Jesus' reminder was that there's no way home to heaven without taking up our cross daily, with his promise and power to get us there.

Despite every desire of my heart to curl up in a ball and go to bed until the baby was born, this wouldn't be a faith-filled following of Jesus. God calls us to an active kind of waiting, which looks like following him in faith despite it sometimes feeling impossible to do so. Faith follows. How can we say we trust Jesus if we refuse to follow him when the load feels too much, or when we feel we can do it on our own? Doesn't God know the load we're carrying, both because he's given it to us and because he's carried it himself, in Jesus? Perhaps this baby would die, a cross so unbearable that it would surely crush me under its weight. But if I'd known that Edith would die, this too would have seemed like an unbearable burden, and yet God had carried us to this point. Wouldn't he do it again?

Despite constant prayer, there was no time when our cross felt any lighter. In the first trimester, morning sickness provided a spurious barometer of the health of the baby. If I was feeling sick, my body was sustaining life, but when I felt better, was it giving up? I was scared of going to the loo in case I'd find blood – a curious first-trimester detail from Edith's pregnancy that I've always looked back on with questions. Much of the second trimester, I longed to feel sick again. Without sickness or movement, how did I know that the baby hadn't just died? How long would it take for my body to tell me? Was this normal ligament pain or should I call a midwife? The questions kept coming, and yet it wasn't until twenty-nine weeks that our worst fears seemed to be coming true.

As I waited for Jonny to pick up the phone, it felt like I couldn't breathe. Was it all happening again? I paced up and down the living room as the ringing tone went on for what felt like an eternity.

'Joanna?' he picked up, about to hear the worst, as he had done every time I'd called him since I was pregnant. But this time he got the response he'd always feared – the unintelligible overflow of crying and fear and breathlessness that made conversation impossible.

'My love, you have to calm down so you can tell me what's going on. Have we lost the baby? Please, Lord, please tell me we've not lost the baby. Joanna?'

But he was talking to himself.

'Joanna, take deep breaths . . . *deep* breaths,' he repeated. I sat myself down on the sofa and breathed in and out, before finally the black mist of panic began to lift.

'We've not lost the baby.' Jonny said nothing, but I heard his relief breathing itself out down the phone. 'Bubs is still moving, but I've had some blood. I've called the Women's Hospital and they've told me to come in.'

'I'll be there as soon as I can,' he replied quickly, putting down the phone.

We were used to waiting hours in triage but it was clear that, with my history, no-one was taking any chances: we were called through right away. Although I'd felt the baby move, this was the first time I'd been in this scenario since I'd been strapped up with Edith and the Doppler stick had been pressed into my side, amplifying nothing more than the faint sounds of my own digestive system. As the midwife picked up the Doppler Jonny turned away, head in hands, unable to cope with what we might find out.

'There's the heartbeat!' the midwife smiled, as she moved the stick towards the bottom of my bump. Jonny looked like he was about to faint, but seemingly there was nothing at all wrong with the baby.

This triggered the first of many bi-weekly scans, Day Assessment Unit visits and pregnancy groups, and as we drew closer to thirty-seven weeks the emotions ramped up. We now knew this little one would survive on the outside, so shouldn't we just get Bubs out? It would have been risky, and perhaps a decision that would undermine God's work to bring us to a greater trust in him. Besides, our consultant didn't like the idea.

By this stage, I was no longer working out how to take the next step, but I was walking – stumbling, at least – down the path God had put me on under the weight of this cross. At each of our multiple scans, rather than being shocked that my baby had once died I was shocked that God had kept this child alive. Here was another life that God had 'fearfully and wonderfully made'. My inability to do anything to sustain my baby's life had previously led to anxious prayer but now, seeing little legs kick the uterus wall and hearing the bloodstream through the placenta, I was drawn to worship . . . and peace. Not peace that rid me of all my fears, but a settled confidence in God and a relief that I was a mere bystander in the whole thing. From my inability to keep this baby alive to my incapability of walking under the burden of this cross, I'd seen God be true to his word – we are dependent on him for life and breath. On the way home to heaven, yes, we're called to walk, but we're also called to watch. To watch God as he proves faithful to his promise to uphold his children as we wait patiently for our hope.

God gives us more than we can carry so that his grace can be seen for what it is: not only as that which saves us, but also as that which upholds us under the many crosses he calls his people to carry – childlessness, baby loss, baby *losses* being some of the burdens he places on our shoulders. And I'm happy he does it this way; after all, the pressure to be able to carry this weight alone would surely be too much. Instead, like Jesus who endured the cross 'for the joy that was set before him' (Hebrews 12:2), by placing these crosses on our shoulders and teaching us to depend on him, he increases our joy as we see his kingdom on the horizon. So long as the joy set before me was the safe delivery of this baby, I was paralysed. But this eternal joy is what has kept me walking under the burden of not knowing whether this pregnancy will end in delight or disaster.

The Lord gives, and he takes away. While I'm desperate that this time he'll give and not take away, the day is coming when God will no longer take away. And that's enough to keep one step in front of the other.

Jonny

It was now late. Joanna lay propped up in her hospital bed, obviously frustrated that the pessary hadn't kickstarted labour.

'Go and get some food,' she said, flicking indiscriminately through a *Hello!* magazine. 'It could be a long night . . .' she mumbled, looking up at me over the magazine. I smiled and turned towards the window. Across the courtyard, the light in Abby Suite 2 was still on. Unable to process the scale of what had happened in our lives since we'd sat in that room, I was happy for the mundane conversation.

'Toby texted to say that they've made enough food for me if I want to drop by for an hour or so. Would you be OK on your own if I did that?'

Joanna smiled. 'That's fine . . . I don't think this baby's budging any time soon.' I smiled and kissed her forehead, turning to leave the ward. Pushing through the double doors, I walked through triage, where the same anxious-looking women sat next to their partners, holding their bumps, under the glow of a TV programme that no one was watching. Thinking of what could lie ahead for any one of those couples filled me with fear. When we'd sat there fourteen months ago with Joanna holding her bump, trying to ignore the daytime TV, we could never have imagined the road ahead. The trauma, the funeral, the grief. The longing, the emptiness, the grief. The anticipation, the fear and the common denominator – the grief.

Turning the corner, excited grandparents walked down the corridor holding an identical balloon to the one I'd seen fourteen months ago – a pink 'It's a girl!' globe, bobbing along on a length of ribbon. Perhaps ours would be a girl. In any case, ours *was* a girl – a beautiful baby girl, who can never be replaced. Whether this one was a boy or a girl, there will always be someone missing from our dinner table; I'll always buy one too few ice creams; we'll always have one child too few.

I crossed the busy road in front of Birmingham Women's Hospital and got into my car. The roads were quiet and wet. The raindrops on my windscreen seemed to dance with energy before being wiped off by the intermittent wipers. The drops began to dance again and then got wiped off. Dance . . . gone. Dance . . . gone.

The Lord gives, and he takes away. Blessed be the name of the Lord.

In the safety and solitude of my car, tears began to form in the corners of my eyes. I wasn't sad but I wasn't happy either. Perhaps they were tears of hope, but they were also tears of grief. Sometimes it's unhelpful to draw such clear divides between the two.

My phone, lying on the dashboard, vibrated violently, piercing the profound moment. I pulled over to check that it was nothing important – a habit formed over the previous eight months.

It was Joanna. 'Please come back. I think it's starting.'

'Resignation' (Part 2)

by Henry Wadsworth Longfellow

In that great cloister's stillness and seclusion,
By guardian angels led,
Safe from temptation, safe from sin's pollution,
She lives, whom we call dead.

Day after day we think what she is doing
In those bright realms of air;
Year after year, her tender steps pursuing,
Behold her grown more fair.

Thus do we walk with her, and keep unbroken
The bond which nature gives,
Thinking that our remembrance, though unspoken,
May reach her where she lives.

Not as a child shall we again behold her;
For when with raptures wild
In our embraces we again enfold her,
She will not be a child;

But a fair maiden, in her Father's mansion,
Clothed with celestial grace;
And beautiful with all the soul's expansion
Shall we behold her face.

And though at times impetuous with emotion
And anguish long suppressed,
The swelling heart heaves moaning like the ocean,
That cannot be at rest,

We will be patient, and assuage the feeling
We may not wholly stay;
By silence sanctifying, not concealing,
The grief that must have way.[6]

10

I will go to her

Joanna

Jonny had said goodbye and drawn the privacy curtain around my bay only for it to be reopened almost immediately. Sarah, the midwife, popped her head through and smiled.

'Time for your second pessary, sweetie!' she beamed, stepping through the curtain and stretching some latex gloves over her hands. We'd met Sarah a few times at check-ups, so it was nice to see a familiar face. Then again, after so many appointments, it felt like we were on first-name terms with most of the hospital staff. There was one midwife, however, whom we'd grown particularly close to.

'Have you heard from Mikaela?' asked Sarah, stepping over discarded jumpers and trashy magazines. 'She's messaging me every two minutes, telling me to give you the biggest sweep of my life, or anything else to get labour started! I think she's nervous . . .'

'Poor girl . . .' I replied. 'I messaged her a minute ago to say the first pessary hadn't really done anything.'

'Well, her shift starts in half an hour so let's hope this one does the trick.' As Sarah prepared the pessary, I distracted myself by thinking about the roundness – the near-completeness – of the situation. We'd met Mikaela hours before she delivered Edith. We'd stood together by Edith's grave. We'd laughed over evening meals and cried about what we'd experienced together in Delivery Room 11. She was the first person we'd told about this pregnancy, and now she was on her way to do it again. We couldn't imagine not having Mikaela deliver this child, or being in any other delivery room. There was a loop that somehow needed to be closed there – a cliffhanger to a story that needed to be resolved.

Sarah peeled off her gloves and discarded them in the clinical waste bin, while I rearranged the thin hospital duvet over my legs.

'Do the second pessaries normally get things going?' I asked, knowing what her answer would be.

'Every woman's different, darling . . . Some get going before they even have their first.' Sarah stopped and turned to me at the bay curtain, and she sighed sympathetically. 'Others have the full three rounds and baby just won't budge.' She smiled again, and drew the curtain shut.

I'll be one of those women, I thought. Lying back on my polyester pillow, I felt emotionally full. *This won't work for me. I'll have my three rounds, and then baby'll die. Something will go wrong . . .* Since finding out I was pregnant, I'd never let myself believe this could possibly end with the joy of new life. I simply didn't believe, despite all the evidence protruding from my tummy, that I'd ever leave this hospital carrying a baby. By closing the door of Abby Suite 2 on my child, I was closing the door on childbirth.

Was this unbelief? Was I doubting God's good character to give good gifts? Or was it disbelief, a way to protect myself from having my heart crushed again?

I could relate readily to Jesus' disciple, Thomas, when he said, 'Unless I see the nail marks in his hands and put my finger where the nails were, and put my hand into his side, I will not believe' (John 20:25). He's gone down as 'Doubting Thomas', but doesn't 'Loving Thomas' do him more justice? The disciple who loved Jesus so much that even to contemplate him being alive felt too painful for the agony it would cause if it weren't true?

Unless I have a baby in my arms, and can hear his breath, and see his chest moving up and down, I will not believe . . . This labour will never start.

But then, it did.

Jonny

'I will go to him' (2 Samuel 12:23). After Joanna had given birth to Edith, these five words brought huge comfort, to confirm what I instinctively knew: that Edith was with God. But while King David's boy had just died, David's calmness does not stem from his assurance about his son's salvation – he assumed that – but rather stems from his assurance about his own salvation. He's not shaking his fist at God or doubting his goodness: he simply looks at his attendants and calmly asserts that, one day, God will take him to that same place.

Who would doubt David's assurance? For God's people, isn't this just basic belief? We are sure of our salvation because of Jesus' death. And yet, to be honest, David's confidence confounds me. Here's a man whose poetry reveals a life built on God and the hope of heaven, but didn't his son's death make him doubt the goodness of the God he'd staked every-thing on? The baby boy was conceived after an adulterous one-night stand. How could he be so sure that God would still welcome him into his kingdom? David writes about how all humanity are sinners from conception, deserving of God's judgment. Didn't he ask himself, even for one moment, whether his boy actually was experiencing God's eternal favour? Do babies *really* go to heaven? Would he? How is David so calm and confident?

David's response is unnerving because it reveals my deepest insecurities. I know that God's Word says that Edith is with Jesus and that, one day, God will take me there too. But my faith is so often characterized by fear, not faith. *This won't work for me. Something will go wrong.* Or worse: *has it worked for Edith?*

I'm like the desperate dad who falls at Jesus' feet with his sick son: 'I believe; help my unbelief!' (Mark 9:24, ESVUK). I'm like Doubting Thomas: if only I could see and touch Edith in glory and know that I will be there too, this would be OK . . . if God somehow revealed this *for sure,* then I could be confident like David. To many, like me, King David may well come across as somewhere between stoically subhuman and spiritually superhuman. But in fact God's king was neither.

David simply took God at his word. Our disbelief that God would give us another baby was understandable because he hadn't promised to do so. But Jesus *did* promise that his kingdom belonged to little ones. God *has* promised to wipe away the very worst sins of the very worst sinners, through simple, childlike faith in Jesus. He *has* promised to bring us to be with him, and with Edith, for eternity – a promise sealed in the blood of his Son, no less. I might be able to articulate these promises, but David's response reveals a man shaped by them, and his response has shaped me in turn. 'I will go to him' isn't wishful thinking or spiritual overconfidence; it's the response of someone who has listened and received God's promises for what they are. They are unfailingly and eternally trustworthy.

Jesus has died and risen to win eternal life for his people, including David's baby boy, our little girl and every other little soul who has gone directly to be with the Lord. My hope doesn't depend on my confidence being as strong as David's, but on the God who has promised it, the God who doesn't, and cannot, lie. So I can share in David's confidence, fixing my eyes on that place which Edith is already enjoying. It might be with a faltering faith and a crushed heart, but still I can say, 'I will go to her. I will see Edith again.'

Joanna

'I'm here, I'm here,' boomed that reassuring West-country voice, before the privacy curtain was tugged open. Mikaela was wearing full-body scrubs, as if I'd just arrived in an emergency ambulance. She stooped down and gave me a hug.

'Hello,' I said, just as Jonny also pulled open the curtain and fixed me with worried eyes.

'Are you OK?' he asked. 'I shouldn't have left you. I shouldn't have . . .' But he stopped mid-sentence as he saw me wince. My womb tightened and an unmistakeable surge of pain left me fumbling for my birthing ball.

'She's doing fine,' Mikaela interjected. 'And you'll be pleased to know that Delivery Room 11 has just become free.' She turned and put her hand on Joanna's lower back. 'We'll bring your stuff, Joanna – are you ready to go through?'

Walking into Room 11 was like walking into a memory – a video tape, filed in the recesses of my mind. That same hot air sat heavily on my shoulders. The gentle pinks morphed into dulcet blues, dancing on the darkened walls above the birthing pool. The aromatherapy fan calmly diffused Edith's lavender scent across the room. The corner sofa stood to attention dutifully.

Like some kind of museum exhibit, the room felt as though it had been left untouched since I'd last walked out of its door and into Abby Suite 2, as though the offence of what had happened here hung heavy in the air and needed correction – redemption, even. I wasn't looking for a successful rerun to make it right. I simply wanted to be in this place because it was a precious memory. This was where we'd welcomed our baby girl into the world with the deepest grief, and now the opportunity to welcome another baby into the same space, this time with unbridled joy, felt too good to pass up. We wanted to resolve the cliffhanger. But Delivery Room 11 felt surprisingly mundane. It was too real – too *earthly* – to bear the weight of significance that my memory had ascribed to it. If I could find some redemption of my pain anywhere in this world, some resolution to this story, it'd be here, under these circumstances. And yet it eluded me.

Jonny arranged indoor candles around my birthing ball, and I plugged into my own thoughts with earphones. As though swimming through deep water, cello strings and piano melodies muffled the sound of my contractions. While the pain continued to surge, a kind of stupor descended, blurring the lines between this labour and the last one. The same

portions of God's Word as when giving birth to Edith un-
furled themselves again:

> We know that the whole creation has been groaning as
> in the pains of childbirth right up to the present time.
> Not only so, but we ourselves, who have the firstfruits of
> the Spirit, groan inwardly as we wait eagerly for our
> adoption to sonship, the redemption of our bodies.
> (Romans 8:22–23)

Groaning in labour when I'd given birth to death was a
powerful picture of my longing for redemption. But now the
scars on my soul groaned even more deeply for healing – for
a redemption and resolution that even this parallel labour
under better circumstances simply could not serve up. Our
story of baby loss simply couldn't be resolved here, and in a
moment of out-of-body clarity I was OK with a cliffhanger,
because I knew the story's ending. From the recesses of my
memory, God kept bringing his Word to mind:

> I consider that our present sufferings are not worth com-
> paring with the glory that will be revealed in us. For the
> creation waits in eager expectation for the children of
> God to be revealed.
> (Romans 8:18–19)

I'd read this verse countless times – I'd held on to it when
giving birth to Edith – although in that moment I *lived* it. The
physical pain I was enduring would be gone the moment this
child appeared. How much more my spiritual groans, when
the children of God are revealed in glory? Only there could

this story be completed and the loop closed, the redemption of both body and soul. After all, how could I expect to find a suitable ending to this story so long as Edith was still gone? But on that day when I will go to her, the intricacies of God's mysterious plan to twist my suffering into his grand narrative of salvation will be made clear. As the cello and piano melodies ramped up towards their crescendo, it was as if the company of heaven were my witness; redemption wasn't here, but it was coming soon.

Mikaela waited for the wince in my eyes to wane before taking my hand to help me into the birthing pool. Just like God's children, I knew this baby was close. Holding on to the side, my legs trembled in the water as I struggled to find an outlet for the pain soaring through my lower body. But because the baby was coming – because God's kingdom was on its way – the pain was worth it. And in that moment, I felt, perhaps for the first time, joy – that heavenly deposit, upholding me through the pain.

Jonny knelt on the floor in front of me, holding his head in his hands. He looked at me deeply, tears flowing. The orchestra's crescendo in my ears was in full swing as my pelvis seemed to break, but I looked at him and my only response was to smile. I really was OK. In the middle of the most overbearing pain, new life was coming. We were so close now.

With one final gasp and groan, I felt a torrent of agony suddenly subside and the weight of life fall from me. As I pulled the music from my ears my spiritual stupor evaporated, and I felt Mikaela reaching to pull the baby out of the water.

'What have you got?!' cried Mikaela. 'Jonny, tell her what you've got!'

Jonny's eyes were scrunched into his face and he removed his glasses. I reached for the pool seat behind me as Mikaela handed me our baby.

'It's a girl,' Jonny whispered through tears. *'Joanna, it's Halle.'*

Unable to feel or speak, I placed her warm body against my chest, and the *beat, beat, beat* that I'd always seen on the screen now merged seamlessly with my own. Each beat was worth a lifetime of labour, each cry better than the crescendo of orchestras the world over. The words didn't flow but they finally came. 'The Lord gives, and he takes away,' I whispered under my breath. 'Blessed be the name of the Lord.'

Jonny

Sometimes I wonder what our lives would look like now if Edith hadn't died. I can picture the scene – in fact I do, nearly every day. Edith would now be walking around our home, calling me 'Dada', throwing chunks of bread from her high chair. Her big brother would be his ever-affectionate self, but learning how to share his toys. We'd be teaching her not to pull her brother's hair, and she'd be learning how to say sorry. She'd be joining in groups at church and starting to under-stand her bedtime Bible stories. She'd put her hands together and say, 'Thank you God for Jesus.'

Had Edith not died, our marriage would never have felt the weight of shared grief or experienced the tension of being pulled in opposite directions. Josiah would never have had his three-year-old mind troubled with questions that many adults struggle with: 'Why did Edith die, Daddy?' or 'When will I see Jesus and Edith, Mama?' Life would have been simple. So it's hardly surprising, that the moment tragedy strikes, the question we all ask is: 'Why would God allow this to happen?'

While I don't and – this side of God's renewed world – will never have definitive answers, I know this: if Edith hadn't died, my worship, love and affections for God would have remained stagnant – lukewarm, as the Bible describes this. Had Edith not died, we would never have experienced Jesus' own hands and feet in the church, holding us up in our grief. We'd never have learned to forgive so readily those who let us down. We'd still have little idea about what it means truly to depend on God in prayer. Above all, we'd never have learned that we can lose everything without losing anything at all, that we can be left with nothing and still have everything in Jesus. We'd still be talking about joy and yet be strangers to it.

God didn't create us for suffering; he created us for worship. But in a fallen world, suffering and *false* worship reign. This God, however, has taken our suffering and repurposed it for the all-satisfying reason for which we were created. Before Edith died, we'd heard that God only does what is right and that he never lets any pain go to waste. But now we know that to be true. Only after experiencing perhaps the worst thing that will happen to us in our lives can I know with confidence that God has never abandoned me this side of heaven – and he never will. Even if worse is to come, I now *know* that:

> neither death nor life, neither angels nor demons, neither the present nor the future, nor any powers, neither height nor depth, nor anything else in all creation, will be able

to separate us from the love of God that is in Christ
Jesus our Lord.
(Romans 8:38–39)

'If God is for us, who can be against us?' writes the apostle
Paul (Romans 8:31). 'He who did not spare his own Son, but
gave him up for us all – how will he not also, along with him,
graciously give us all things?' (8:32). This God, who was
willing to experience the loss of a child himself, is the God
who has only given Edith what is good for her and, even in the
pain left in her wake, has only ever used it to do good for us,
in us and through us. If Edith hadn't died, God would have
withheld these good things – something his love for us, and
for Edith, would simply not allow him to do.

Often I lie awake thinking about what Edith looks like in
glory – does she still have auburn hair and reddened lips?
I don't know what it will be like when we meet again in that
place. *Will I recognize her? Will she know who I am? Will she
know that I never wanted anything other than to protect her?
Did she see it when I closed the door of Abby Suite 2, leaving
her to the care of others? Did she feel my heart break for her,
and the fatherly love I longed to lavish on her? Will we laugh or
will we cry when we meet? Has Joanna's mum told her all about
us – how we longed to have her . . . how we longed to chase her
round the garden and teach her about Jesus? How I longed to
walk her down the aisle?*

  Edith's life in glory is shrouded in mystery. But, as an echo
of King David's confidence, I know this: Edith and I will be
united in love – yes, for each other, but united more supremely
in our perfect love for the Lord Jesus Christ.

In a loud voice they were saying:
  'Worthy is the Lamb, who was slain,
    to receive power and wealth and wisdom
      and strength
    and honour and glory and praise!'
(Revelation 5:12)

I may picture redemption as being when I take my little girl by the hand and look deeply into her eyes. But redemption will be when I stand hand in hand with my daughter, with raised hands in praise of God our Saviour. I will see what Edith has always seen; I will see God face to face, and 'he will wipe every tear away from our eyes' and, in that place, 'there will be no more death or mourning or crying or pain' (Revelation 21:4). Yes, I will see and love my daughter. But above all, I will see his face – the God who only did good to me – and I will love him for ever.

Joanna

The smell of the ward had become homely . . . safe, perhaps. It was hard to tell. On the bed, Jonny had arranged my suitcase, the maternity bag and Halle's car seat.

'You ready?' he said, taking me by the hand. 'I'll carry the little one – you've carried her for eight months.'

On the way out, walking past the delivery ward, I turned and looked down the corridor, beyond Delivery Room 11. The door to Abby Suite 2 was still displaying its 'In Use' sign. Slowly it opened and a man stepped out. He turned his back, making sure the door didn't slam behind him, before walking off in the opposite direction.

'No way,' Jonny whispered in disbelief. 'Joanna, that was the man I worked with in our pregnancy class. You often chatted to his wife . . .'

My head sank into my chest and adrenaline swelled. I wanted to run after him and hug him and tell him that his daughter was safe; but my feet felt glued to the sticky, blue linoleum floor. And he was gone.

'I can't believe it . . . last week her daughter was doing huge kicks, and now . . . I just . . . I can't . . .' I turned to look at Jonny, and behind him on the walls were pictures of matrons, shift leaders and trainee midwives, whose beaming smiles we'd walked past so often. But for the first time they seemed to jar. *Was this a place where we should be smiling?*

As we moved towards the lobby, women walked in every direction holding pregnancy notes, midwives laughed off the pressures of long shifts over coffee, and Jeremy Kyle's voice provided a distant TV backing track. Still reeling from what we'd just seen, something about the cheery hubbub failed to communicate the sombre and complex emotions soaked into these walls over the decades.

Yes, this was a place of happiness, where we look at ultrasound screens with amazement and where we meet our babies for the first time. But as I looked around at the glow on everyone's face, the superficiality screamed loudly. Where were the parents heading off to the Early Pregnancy Unit for an emergency scan? Where were the single mums bringing in the remains of their miscarried children under doctors' orders? Where were the fearful dads who'd just heard that their babies showed signs of fatal anomalies? Who was talking about the abortion clinic three storeys above us? Where were the tears of parents who'd just heard the words: 'I'm sorry, I can't find a heartbeat'?

By now I knew the stats; I knew that a large proportion of women here had experienced, or would experience, the loss of a baby at some point. Pain all around me, and yet I couldn't see it. The silent cries of baby-loss sufferers were hidden away on one small ward and its little Grief Garden.

From the outside, I was only contributing to the buy-out bustle of enthusiastic mums. Indeed, holding my newborn, I'd got to the place all these excited parents were heading for. They couldn't see the wounds that I carried out of this hospital fourteen months ago, which had barely begun to heal, even with a newborn in my arms. I was just part of the many here whose silent cries were siphoned off by socially acceptable smiles.

And this was just one day, in one hospital, in one city, in one country of the world. But in every family and workplace, church and mosque, town and village, all across the globe, tears were being suppressed, and if we caught them surely the oceans would provide too small a vessel.

Can I really believe in a God who is in control of such a massacre? But my question is rather: how do grieving parents continue without holding on to the promises of God? If there weren't a real and glorious place into which all these hundreds of millions of souls were brought, I certainly couldn't cope, or continue. But we've seen how Jesus rose from the dead in order to raise us and our little ones to new life. This place is real, physical and *near*. Not one of those souls has been lost, and so I put my hope in God because there's no hope besides him – and because he only does good, even when we can't see it or sense it.

I looked down at Halle in her car seat as we walked out into the cold. It was a blustery November day and the bare trees swung wildly. The scene reminded me of the familiar words that we had read to Edith before leaving her: 'In the winter it looks like the trees have all died. Their leaves wither and drop off.'

'This is the world, little girl,' Jonny said. 'It's not always winter, though; in a few months, spring will be on its way.' I rehearsed what was imprinted on my memory: 'It looks dead, but the buds are ready to go and, come spring, they will blossom fruit!'

Epilogue

We all like stories with happy endings. Or at least, those ones where every thread has been neatly resolved, with none left dangling. But after writing about grief that will never wholly leave us, to finish the story in that neat and tidy way would undermine our message.

Halle's birth seemed the right place to draw this book to a close, not because it marked the end of our grief but because it has led to a new chapter for our family. But, as we write, Halle is eight months old and what we once understood from a distance is now a reality: grief never goes away.

Even since submitting the first manuscript of this book, a few months ago, the effects of losing Edith continue in our daily lives. We have experienced new shadows cast by *that day* which will shape the rest of our lives: disturbing visions, physical shaking, panic attacks, sleep disturbance and other widely accepted symptoms of trauma. A pastor at church has led us through counselling. Only this morning, a GP referred us to a specialist, with suspected post traumatic stress disorder.

Perhaps this feels like a discouraging way to end a book. But in the light of your own possible grief, wouldn't it be more discouraging to give the impression that we've now risen above this? That we've conquered the past and can launch forwards, leaving other grieving parents behind? This would move our story into the realm of fairy tale. After all, our main aim in writing this was to communicate the hope that is found in Jesus Christ alone – not to tick off the stages of some neatly mapped-out grief process, or announce another baby, or anything else. It's for this reason that we've chosen to conclude the book in this way, not as a happy-ever-after but with the details of the turbulent and traumatic days that followed the book's completion. And because our hope is in Jesus alone and the new world he has promised us, we don't need to hide behind pretences of victory or be embarrassed that we don't have any silver-bullet coping strategies. What we do have we have held out to you: *we have Jesus*. We have the promise of the Father's love and presence through the storm. We have a future of unending joy – the joy our children are experiencing now. This trumps the best of coping strategies. Our future in him is far greater than present healing. He is all we need.

Perhaps you were hoping for more. Maybe you thought that reading this book would heal some of the pain – maybe it has done, in small part, and if so we are pleased. Either way, there is a sure hope of healing in God's coming kingdom, and peace knowing that it is God himself who will keep us safe in his embrace until we get there. This is what we're most prone to forget, yet it's the very truth that keeps us plodding on towards that day.

May God bless you, as you stay close to him over the coming months, years and decades. The happy ending will come; winter will soon end, thawed by eternity's glow.

Edith Joy Adeah Ivey – Abby Suite 2

Jonny, Joanna, Josiah and Halle Ivey

Notes

1 'Sun and moon' by Ben Moore, used by permission.
2 From 'Winter' by Sally Lloyd-Jones, in *Thoughts to Make Your Heart Sing*, Sally Lloyd-Jones and Jago. Zondervan, 2012. Copyright © Sally Lloyd-Jones and Jago, 2021, used by permission of Zondervan.
3 From 'Winter' by Sally Lloyd-Jones, in *Thoughts to Make Your Heart Sing*, Sally Lloyd-Jones and Jago. Zondervan, 2012. Copyright © Sally Lloyd-Jones and Jago, 2021, used by permission of Zondervan.
4 'We rest on Thee', words by Edith Gilling Cherry (1872–1897).
5 From 'Resignation' by Henry Wadsworth Longfellow (from Maine Historical Society, available online at: <www.hwlongfellow.org>, accessed 15 October 2020).
6 From 'Resignation' by Henry Wadsworth Longfellow (from Maine Historical Society, available online at: <www.hwlongfellow.org>, accessed 15 October 2020).